The 250 QUESTIONS EVERY SELF-EMPLOYED Person Should Ask

Published by Adams Business, an imprint of Adams Media,
a division of F+W Media, Inc.
57 Littlefield Street, Avon, MA 02322. U.S.A.
www.adamsmedia.com

ISBN 10: 1-60550-640-0
ISBN 13: 978-1-60550-640-1

Printed in the United States of America.

10 9 8 7 6 5 4 3 2 1

Library of Congress Cataloging-in-Publication Data
is available from the publisher.

This publication is designed to provide accurate and authoritative information
with regard to the subject matter covered. It is sold with the understanding
that the publisher is not engaged in rendering legal, accounting, or other professional advice. If legal advice or other expert assistance is required, the services of a competent professional person should be sought.
　　—From a *Declaration of Principles* jointly adopted by a Committee of the
American Bar Association and a Committee of Publishers and Associations

Many of the designations used by manufacturers and sellers to distinguish
their products are claimed as trademarks. Where those designations appear in
this book and Adams Media was aware of a trademark claim, the designations
have been printed with initial capital letters.

*This book is available at quantity discounts for bulk purchases.
For information, call 1-800-289-0963.*

The 250 QUESTIONS EVERY SELF-EMPLOYED Person Should Ask

MARY MIHALY

BUSINESS

Avon, Massachusetts

For my sisters, Carol Sue
and Margaret Ann,
who never let me fall.

CONTENTS

Introduction   xi

PART 1

The Decision and Getting Started   1

PART 2

The Office   29

PART 3

Financial and Legal Aspects   43

PART 4

**Marketing and Selling Your Products
and Services**   71

PART 5

Time, Energy, and Personal Considerations   103

PART 6

Managing Ongoing Success   119

Afterword   147
Appendix A: Sample Contract   149
Appendix B: The 250 Questions   151

Index   173

ACKNOWLEDGMENTS

A dear family friend, Nancy Carney, used to say that if she ever wrote a book, she would list 5,000 people in the Acknowledgements. That way, she would sell at least 5,000 books because they all would buy one.

While I don't have quite that many names in my Rolodex (yes, I still use one of those), I do need to mention a few friends and champions without whose nurturing support I would be adrift, especially when I'm pulling together a book.

Every self-employed person needs to surround herself with a solid infrastructure of expertise; mine would collapse without my accountant, Steve Wagner, who teaches me something new each time we talk; my agent, Bob Diforio, whose confidence in me I deeply appreciate; and my editor, Peter Archer, who made my job easier—and this book infinitely more useful for readers—with his sharp eye. I'm grateful for Peter's patience and belief in this project.

Without the persistent friendship of Marael Johnson, Mike Kristan, and Patrick Lewis, I'm not sure I would finish anything. Cheryl Hudecek, you rescued my sanity one day when I was dangling; I owe you. And Roberto, well, you're just as enduring as the universe, aren't you. Keith Brown, all those lifetimes—no wonder we finish each other's sentences. Sandy Lamb—Sis—your business smarts and generosity of heart are constants; you know I depend on you.

Any wisdom in this book was channeled from my friends and colleagues in the American Society of Journalists and Authors (ASJA). They are my community of self-employed stars.

INTRODUCTION

As a child of the 1960s and daughter of a self-employed accountant, I grew up believing that self-employed people were the backbone of America. Small businesses—those with an owner and perhaps an assistant or two—defined commerce in this country's earliest years, and they still drive much of our economy. According to the U.S. Census Bureau, the number of "non-employer businesses," or those owned by self-employed people, grew from 15.4 million to nearly 21 million between 1997 and 2006. Another 4.5 million businesses had three employees or less in 2005. That's a pretty wide independent streak.

Almost everyone dreams of owning their own business. Whether you want to provide a service—design brochures, groom puppies, sell real estate, or drive a taxi—or manufacture products, today's self-employed people have much in common with each other. Unlike entrepreneurs who came before, who may have been the only typewriter repairmen or flower arrangers in their towns, contemporary independents have competition. Thanks to the Internet, home offices now have a presence in nearly every industry. That means, you—as a self-employed person—regardless of your occupation, must learn marketing skills, and then get out there and promote yourself. The marketplace of the self-employed individual used to be their town square or bedroom community, but today, home-based businesses can market to the world.

Your reasons for becoming your own boss may be diverse: you may be pursuing a passion, or could be ready to leave an unpleasant workplace situation. You may have just recognized that you work best alone and, while you aren't sure what your new enterprise will be, you know you want to work for yourself, in your own company. *The 250 Questions Every Self-Employed Person Should Ask* will clear the fog surrounding such efforts as marketing plans and virtual assistants, and explain why self-employed people need to expand their visions and embrace new skills. You will learn the pros and cons of buying a franchise, why you need a succession plan, and what to include in an employee handbook. From the initial decision to work for yourself through setting up a home office, keeping the Internal Revenue Service happy, and snagging new clients—even in tough times—you will find information to help your businesses thrive.

You'll note that throughout this book, I often refer to a "small business" or "small business owner." Generally, I use that phrasing to describe a self-employed person who employs one or more staff. Technically, a self-employed author working in a home office, such as myself, also is a small businessperson. But the popular notion of "small business" is the corner dry cleaner, or a boutique, or some other establishment that employs at least two or three people. The owner of such a small business most definitely is a self-employed person, and this book is for him or her as well as for home-based consultants, editors, designers, and others lucky enough to earn a living working independently from a home office.

I also often use the word "entrepreneur" interchangeably with "self-employed person." If you have started (or plan to start) your own business, or whether you work independently or hire assistants or other staff, you fit the "entrepreneur" tag and this book is for you.

I wish this book had been available when I first committed to self-employment. I was the poster girl for naiveté. How else to explain my insistence that I would never have a boss again? Little did I know that, once I entered client-land, I would have at least a dozen "bosses" at any given time. Everyone is accountable to someone, and self-employed people are no exception.

That was my first surprise. The second was learning that I wasn't as independent as I had assumed I would be. I was never a "joiner," so I believed there was no reason for me to join any trade associations, societies, or other groups whose members, I thought, obviously couldn't make it on their own. What nonsense. It took me years to understand that self-employed people are stronger when they speak with one voice, and that there were immense benefits waiting for me in those groups. Today, my associations and networking through the American Society of Journalists and Authors, Society of American Travel Writers, and The Authors Guild, among others, has literally put tens of thousands of dollars into my pocket every year.

Financial planning, knowing one's prospective customers, and an honest appraisal of your own work habits, ambitions, capabilities, and shortcomings are key to succeeding as a self-employed person. There are bound to be pitfalls and detours along the way, but the more questions you can anticipate, the greater your potential for long-term success.

We've provided 250 questions to get you started.

PART 1

The Decision and Getting Started

IT'S BEEN ON your mind for some time now, and you're close to deciding that you want to be your own boss—but where do you begin such a complex passage in your life? Part 1 will help you determine, once and for all, whether self-employment is for you.

You'll start by examining your own motivations and skills, and by taking a realistic look at everything you will gain—and relinquish—if you switch to self-employment. This section will help you select a business, evaluate your finances and risk-taking capacity, and realize what sort of professional assistance you might need along the way. If your plans go beyond a home-based business, we've also included information on the ins and outs of franchises, and notes on starting a new enterprise versus buying an existing business. When you finish this section, you will be well equipped to make your final decision—and a commitment!

#1.   **Which personal qualities do I need to be successfully self-employed?**

The hallmark of a self-employed person's life is hard work. No couch potatoes need apply. If you anticipate working shorter days and never putting in weekend hours, you will be disappointed. From marketing to production, whether you're selling resumes or spots in a children's nursery, every small business owner is a hands-on worker. The only way to keep costs down is to do much of the work yourself.

You also should enjoy responsibility. All of the legal, financial, ethical, managerial, and production aspects of your business will land on your desk. When the business thrives, the credit goes to you—but if it tanks, that too will be your responsibility.

Persistence is another key quality. You'll need it to get you through the times when the money runs thin, suppliers aren't delivering, customers are angry, and you want to give up.

Lastly, you will need a reputation for honesty. Businesses are built on relationships, and you can only turn occasional customers and vendors into relationships if the individuals trust you.

#2.   **How do I know if I'm self-motivated enough to be a business owner?**

Notice this is a different question from, *Are you miserable when Monday mornings come around?* and *Are you ready to leave your current job?*

Do you have enough cash saved to pay your personal bills and living expenses for about six months? Because whether you can discipline yourself to save a healthy supply of cash before you begin will be your first self-motivation test.

We mentioned persistence when answering question #1, but it's worth emphasizing here: are you good at finishing what you start? You can't embark on a new business, then quickly tire of it and move on to something else. Check your personality and habits, and be honest with yourself. Can you commit to sticking with the business once you begin?

You also need to motivate yourself to try things that you've never done before. We'll talk about public speaking in Part 4, but you should ask yourself now whether you're willing to get past shyness and put yourself "out there" to make your business succeed. As the business owner, you will be the one spreading the good word about your products or services. If local television stations or newspapers want to talk, you should be ready with enthusiasm, poise, and great things to say about your business!

You could also say that being self-employed is a little bit about being brave.

#3.   Which job benefits will I lose when I become self-employed?

As a person with no "employer" per se, there will be no one to pay for your health insurance. That's probably the most substantial financial benefit you will sacrifice; in 2008 the average annual premium for a family's health insurance was $12,680, according to the Kaiser Family Foundation. The good news for self-employed people is that health cost is a major reason that many companies contract with independent workers instead of hiring full-time employees; they don't pay health insurance for independents. If you're going to be covered, you will pay the premiums under an individual plan.

You also will relinquish non-monetary benefits, such as being part of a corporate family. The isolation of working for yourself is something to consider. Many people blossom and thrive when they're left to themselves, but others crave coworkers and structure. You might even discover that you miss having someone make major work decisions for you!

#4. **What are some financial pluses of being self-employed?**

Lest the message be entirely doom-and-gloom, hear this: the sky is the limit! As a self-employed person, you are not restricted to anyone else's ideas of how much money you should earn, or how often you should give yourself a raise. Go ahead. Make money by the bucketful!

You also will save money in ways that might surprise you. No more monthly parking fees, pricey lunches downtown, obligatory drinks after work, candy and cookies that your coworker's kids are selling, expensive work suits, dry cleaning costs, or constant gasoline fill-ups. And that's before you start tallying up your income tax deductions that didn't exist when you were someone else's employee.

#5. **What are some other advantages of self-employment—especially if I'm working from a home office?**

Your schedule will be flexible. If you need time during the day for banking, exercising, a parent-teacher conference, shopping, or even just a nap on a rainy afternoon, you don't have to ask anyone's permission or make arrangements with coworkers. A few additional bonuses include:

- There is no dress code at home. You can stay in your fuzzy slippers all day—though some of the best advice I received when I first started working for myself was to dress every day as if I were going to the office. I don't take it that far, but I do wear decent pants and sweaters, and always wear shoes. Somehow, I can't get started until I kick off those slippers and put on some shoes. Then I feel as if I'm "going somewhere."

- No more commuting! There is nothing more luxurious than standing at your front window in the dead of winter, a cup of steaming-hot coffee in your hand, as you watch commuters sliding on the icy streets and listen to them scraping ice from their windshields.
- You are no longer bound to the corporate culture. If you didn't trust your employer, or didn't approve of the way he treated customers or even other employees, it is a relief to walk away. From now on, only you will define your corporate culture.
- You will now have time and energy for your family and friends. You'll put in long hours, but you can arrange that time any way you like. You might even find time to read a good novel.
- You'll be your own boss! You can be as creative as you like. Your parameters will be set by you and no one else.

#6.   I want to work from home. How do I decide what kind of business to start?

There are three main points to put into play. First, what are your talents and skills? If you can't cook, don't start a restaurant. If none of your skills stand out, make a list. Do you know how to sew? You could start doing alterations for people. Are you good with older people? Perhaps a nearby nursing home can use your help in some capacity.

Second, what do you know? Have you collected stories about local history? Your community might need someone to hire herself out to local museums, set up exhibits, give tours, and help develop brochures. Do your friends admire your upbeat personality? Maybe local chefs can use your enthusiasm to publicize their tastings and other special events.

Third, produce what will sell. Be creative in finding your niche, but don't choose a calling that's so obscure no one will see the need for it.

#7. What are the most popular home-based businesses?

Almost any kind of professional consulting service is popular among those who want to work from home, including financial counseling, editorial services, travel agenting, antique appraisals, and insurance sales. However, if your consulting business would have clients coming to your home office for appointments, be sure to check with your local zoning commission. If your neighborhood isn't zoned for a public office and a neighbor complains about the traffic traipsing in and out of your house, you can be shut down; it happened to a member of my family, an accountant who had spent a lot of money remodeling his garage into an office.

Other popular home-based businesses are those repair "shops" that don't involve a lot of client traffic or major equipment. Examples of this are computer repair, doll repair, clothing alterations, and costume making. Specialty teaching, too, is a category you might consider if you have knowledge shared by relatively few people. One friend gives talks on Victoriana. Another speaks to school and Elderhostel groups about turtles in her local park system.

#8. How will I know when to quit my day job and start my new business?

We'll discuss business plans and other specific groundwork that will help you launch your business later in this section. Your most immediate concern is likely to be whether you can afford to leave full-time employment and start your own business. To that end, experts recommend setting aside 5 percent of your paycheck until you build enough of a cash reserve to live on for six months. While you're saving money, you can work on your business and marketing plans, and gradually set up your office.

#9. **Is starting a business in a tough economy a bad decision?**

No. If you have studied the market, saved money to cover your living expenses, and planned for every contingency you can think of, tough times can actually work in your favor. It might be a terrific time, in fact, to buy an existing business if you go into it with your eyes open. However, you should learn everything you can about why that business failed and have your own remedies ready.

Consider, too, that if you want to start a new business during an economic slump, your start-up costs may be lower: For instance, if you need to operate out of a storefront you may be able to negotiate better terms on your lease if the owner needs to fill the space. You probably will find great sales on office equipment and furnishings and, if you're stocking shelves, your initial investment in your inventory could be discounted. Your competition may be weakened by a sluggish economy, but while you don't want to celebrate someone else's hardships, you should be alert for new opportunities in your field.

But before you begin, ask yourself if your area needs the service you want to provide. Does your town need another gift shop? In an economic downturn, probably not. Any sort of new (or re-opening) retail enterprise must be seen as a necessity by the community and customer base or it won't succeed.

Looking for investors will also be more challenging in an economic slump. Any capital-heavy business—for instance, a snow-removal operation that requires several trucks and plows, or a bakery that involves leasing or buying a building, ovens, and other expensive equipment—should be viewed as a risk in such times. But if you see a need for the services you offer, especially if employers in your area have downsized employees who perform those services, it can be a good time for you to step up and offer to fill in as an independent contractor.

#10.   **Why do so many people want to run their own businesses?**

For the same reasons you want to run yours. They have a dream, they want to create a legacy for their children, they have a passion they want to follow and work at every day, and they hate having a boss. They want to set their own hours, make their own rules, and develop their own work relationships.

Intuit, the makers of QuickBooks and other business products and services, recently surveyed 1,000 people, ages twenty-five to fifty-five, about starting their own businesses. They learned that about three-quarters of Americans see owning a home or business as the "American Dream," while 84 percent thought that if they started their own business, they would be more passionate about their work. More than a third regretted not starting their own businesses.

Their primary reasons for wanting to start a business include:

- **40 percent** wanted to love their work.
- **24 percent** wanted to be their own boss.
- **21 percent** wanted more flexible schedules.
- **15 percent** wanted to spend more time with their families.

Interestingly, 66 percent of women respondents said they were inspired to succeed in business by Oprah Winfrey—and 34 percent of men said their inspiration was Hugh Hefner!

#11.   **I haven't told my spouse that I want to start my own business and work from home. What issues should I bring up in that conversation?**

No matter how quiet or solitary you imagine your new work life to be, this move will change your lives for years to come. Your entire family will be affected by your decision.

Your spouse's first concern is likely to be financial security. Even if your financial investment is small, your income is sure to be disrupted by starting your own business. Be prepared with facts and figures to assure your partner that any financial setbacks are likely to be short-lived.

Be forthright, too, about the disruption to your home life. Most self-employed people invest fifty to sixty hours a week in their jobs. They work into the evening and on weekends, and cozy breakfasts and leisurely dinners may become rare treats. Schedules may need shifting, chores might be delayed, and paid vacation time is a thing of the past. Anticipate the sacrifices you're asking of your spouse, including time with you.

#12. What is the survival rate for a new small business?

According to the Small Business Administration's Office of Advocacy, the four-year survival rate for nonminority-owned businesses is 72.6 percent. The survival rate is 72.1 percent for Asian-owned businesses, 68.6 percent for Hispanic-owned businesses, 67 percent for Native American and Alaskan businesses, and 61 percent for African American–owned businesses.

Those figures are several years old at this writing, and while they might seem a bit low, previous studies showed survival rates only at 40 to 50 percent! With training, both now and in the past, rates soar as high as 90 percent.

#13. What are the top reasons home-based businesses fail?

Poor planning, financial and otherwise, can be blamed for the majority of home-based businesses that don't survive. Very few people can invent a "pet rock" and make an instant fortune; building security in business is a long process and small businesspeople must prepare themselves for a journey filled with detail work.

If you check the Internet, you'll find thousands of business authors citing reasons why home-based businesses fail. These "Top Five" are mentioned most often:

1. **Poor planning:** You cannot succeed in business without good planning. That's where a formal business plan, which we'll discuss at length later in this section, can literally save your business. The more detailed your plan, the better your chances for surviving and thriving.

2. **Poor marketing:** If you're typically a shy person who isn't comfortable putting herself "out there," get past those fears before you start your business. Clients won't come knocking on the door of your home office; you have to promote yourself constantly in order to establish your business. I know some highly successful self-employed people who do at least one thing to market their business every day—no exceptions; it's that important.

3. **Lack of funds:** For people in home-based businesses, it can be tempting to take a folksy, casual attitude toward money. Many go into debt, even using personal credit cards to start or operate the business, especially in areas such as design or freelance editing that don't require much start-up capital. Instead, start with cash reserves that will take you through six months and keep that reserve in an emergency savings account or, if you're certain you can pay your bills for at least three months, a short-term CD (certificate of deposit) to get you through the rough times. But use caution if you put money into a CD: if you do need the cash sooner than the CD's maturity date, the penalties are brutal.

4. **Impatience:** People working alone often find it difficult to take the "long view," especially when unexpected obstacles crop up, such as clients not paying their bills.

5. **Lack of self-discipline:** It's a rare person who can sustain passion for their work every day, week after week, year after

year. But when clients need your services or product, you must deliver, regardless of whether you feel like working.

And, frankly, some small businesspeople allow their egos to get in their way. No matter how delicious your spaghetti sauce, pasta lovers will find countless other great sauce choices after your company folds. Small business owners need to find a way to show pride in their products and services without being perceived as prima donnas.

#14. **What kind of small business will be successful?**

The kind that is so specialized it's almost rare, and involves training that very few people have undertaken. If you somehow became an expert over the years on the technology of turning soda cans into life-saving medicine, you can bet there are some government officials who want your phone number. Become a specialist in solving some problem that no one (or only a few people) can quite manage, and you will have a very busy consulting practice.

That said, few people are so creative that they will turn heads just by mentioning what they do for a living—but it's critical to differentiate yourself from the crowd, preferably by the quality of your service or product, rather than by using gimmicks. If nothing else, provide some aspect of extraordinary customer service that none of your competitors are offering. Unless you can distinguish yourself from the competition and give clients a real reason to become repeat customers, you will lose your business.

#15. **What is the biggest challenge facing small businesses?**

The financial challenge of working independently tops the list. You're likely to use your own money to launch your business, especially if you start it during a credit crunch. Ask yourself, if the biz isn't successful, can you afford to lose the cash you sank into it and still meet your personal financial obligations without skipping payments? It's important for new business owners to keep all of their financial goals in sight—college savings for the kids, their own retirement, etc.—in addition to their business goals.

#16. **What type of business can I start with little or no capital?**

Think of businesses in which the owner needs little more than a computer, a phone, some desk space, perhaps a stash of supplies, and a filing cabinet. Look at *www.etsy.com*, a wildly popular handicrafts site. Many of the artisans who sell their work on such sites have home-based businesses that need little capital and bring in a full-time income. Jewelry designers, handbag artists, and painters can work from their homes. It's tempting to include professional photographers in the list, but their equipment can run into the tens of thousands of dollars.

Customer service is one of the hottest home-based businesses these days; companies hire people to take inquiries or complaints from customers and either resolve the matter on the phone, or route the question to someone who has the answer. (You didn't think those credit card phone people sat in a posh office all day, did you? Chances are they're sitting in their dining room.) Editorial and travel services are also fields that need little equipment or capital.

Consultants in all sorts of fields can build successful home-based businesses, too. What do you know about? Can you design efficient closet space? Then you could contact a design firm, or one of the box-chain supply stores, and ask about designing storage space for their customers. Do you know about property rights in your community? Make an appointment with your local housing court to see if they would hire you to consult with area landlords. Are you good at helping people make decisions about the future? Look into training to become a life coach.

#17. **I keep hearing about the "informal economy," or "hidden economy." What is that and is it a good way for me to start my self-employment?**

The informal or hidden economy is made up of un-taxed businesses that are largely illegal. However, that doesn't mean their owners are involved in criminal activity, such as selling drugs. On the contrary, they are the unlicensed, seemingly innocent, under-the-table businesses that seem to be everywhere: the fellow down the street who repairs neighbors' cars in his driveway; the woman who babysits four or five children full-time without a license; house cleaning; house repairs; impromptu flea market operators.

However, licenses and regulations exist for our protection. Perhaps the neighbor who babysits, for instance, is quite capable and loves children—but without the right licenses and inspections, do parents know if her backyard swings are safe? For those working in the "underground economy," penalties for operating without permits and failing to report income to the IRS can be steep. A more productive approach is better, more widespread education on legitimate self-employment.

#18. **How much money will I need to start my business?**

There is no single answer to that question. Every business is unique. However, in addition to your savings, you should have the funds to operate every part of your business from the beginning. That includes communications (quality letterhead and business cards, supplies, postage, phone, computer and software with the capacity to do the job), any necessary travel, association dues, fees for an accountant and any other necessary consultants, advertising if appropriate, office furnishings, and an amount set aside to run the business for a month or two in an emergency.

If your new small business is not home-based—say, if you're opening a bakery or a real estate office—then you also will need funds for office space, employees, signage, and equipment.

The topic of startup money, and saving to start your business, will reappear several times in this book, in different contexts. Clearly, it's the biggest concern for everyone who wants to be self-employed!

#19. Where do self-employed people find the money to start their businesses?

An obvious source, especially for a home-based business that needs little start-up capital, is your circle of family and friends. If you approach them, experts offer these tips to make the borrowing process as painless as possible for everyone concerned:

- Approach family and friends whom you know are "risk takers" by nature and be completely honest with them about your plans. Open your books, show them your business and marketing plan, and treat them as partners.
- Don't ask for money from friends or family who can't afford it. If you aren't sure about an individual's financial status, skip that person—or ask someone close to you who knows more. The last thing you want to do is embarrass someone who might help you in the future.
- If you have friends or family who also have friends who might invest, be forthright in asking about those possibilities as well.
- Don't ask friends or family who are almost sure to say "no."
- Behave professionally when you ask for money, even if the person is a sibling. People take their money seriously, and you need them to trust your ability to repay the loan.
- Plan to update all lenders often regarding your progress.

If you plan to borrow less than $10,000, you might be a candidate for a micro loan. Banks have always given micro loans, although they may be reluctant to take risks on a new business if you're asking during an economic downturn. Try credit unions as well.

A borrowing trend that appears here to stay is online peer-to-peer loans. The "investors" are simply people who enjoy lending a hand, and their personal funds, to someone who needs and deserves it. If you can document your credit status and income, they might take a chance on you. Three of the more respected "banks" are *www*
.prosper.com, *www.biz2credit.com*, and *www.lendingclub.com*. An intriguing newcomer is *www.circlelending.com*, part of the Virgin Atlantic corporate family.

#20. **What is the SBA's (Small Business Administration's) start-up loan program, and what can the SBA do for me?**

Formally known as the SBA's Basic 7(a) Loan Program (because it was created by that clause in the federal Small Business Act), the program is carried out by most of the banks and non-bank lenders across the country.

Here's how it works: a business owner (you) applies for a loan with her local lender, who decides if it will make the loan internally, using its own loan funds. If your application has weaknesses the bank will ask the SBA for a guaranty. In effect, the SBA is the co-signer for your loan, which actually comes from the commercial lender, not from the government.

The SBA—created to counsel and assist small businesses— offers help of almost every kind to small business owners, from writing a business plan, which you can find online with detailed instructions, to tips on buying a franchise or other businesses, leasing equipment, managing employees, planning your exit from the company, transferring ownership, and liquidating your assets.

The SBA will even help you choose a name for your new creation. Check out their services at *www.sba.gov*.

#21.   Do I need a mentor, and where would I find one?

The good people at Service Corps of Retired Executives (SCORE), an affiliate of the SBA, practically invented mentoring. And if you want proof that you do need a mentor, consider that Vera Bradley, whose line of women's accessories gets hotter every year, started her business with a mentor from SCORE.

At *www.score.org*, the online tools allow you to select up to ten industries, from dry cleaning to funds and trusts. When you click "Submit," you will receive a list of mentors near your zip code. SCORE's mentors are retired professionals who donate their time and expertise to counsel and coach small business owners.

If you're just starting your business, SCORE recommends consulting with several mentors, depending on your needs—for example, a human resources expert to help you write your employee manual, an accountant to help you understand your bookkeeping needs, and an attorney to help you choose the best corporate structure for your business. Or, you might select a mentor with deep knowledge of your clients' industries, so you can communicate with them more easily.

#22.   Do I need an accountant to start or buy my own business?

Every self-employed person and business owner needs an accountant. Not everyone agrees with that statement, and a sole proprietor—someone who works alone, with no employees—may only need an accountant's services at income tax time. But when you need advice in an area you don't know much about, it's good to have a relationship with someone who knows the answers. Even Douglas H. Shulman, the head of the Internal Revenue Service when this book went to press, engages another accountant for calculating his income tax.

It's important to consult a certified public accountant (CPA), rather than an uncertified accountant, because CPAs must update their credentials and knowledge periodically and requalify for certification.

A CPA is informed not only about recent changes to the tax codes, but also in the subtle ways in which those changes can be interpreted. She knows how to research your questions and continually purchases new software to update her own knowledge. A CPA's services will cost more than those of an uncertified accountant, but her expertise is well worth it. Ask your friends and colleagues who own small businesses for referrals; there are many tax issues that relate to self-employed people and you'll want to work with a CPA who is experienced in working with independent contractors.

#23. **Do I need an attorney in order to start or buy my own business?**

If you are going to be a home-based sole proprietor—a one-person business—then no, you probably don't need to consult an attorney before you go into business. Chances are, your accountant will be able to answer most of your questions. You also will get good advice from mentors and from colleagues in work-related associations, which I highly recommend joining. You will read more about trade associations in Part 5. From those resources, you can get a basic understanding of your legal responsibilities and liabilities, including simple contract agreements you may have to sign with clients.

However, if you plan to enter into major contracts that involve a significant investment on your part, such as a lease for office space or employee contracts, then it would be a good idea to have a relationship with an attorney. Whether you engage him on a retainer basis may depend on how often you will need his services. Again, seek advice from mentors or others whose experience reflects your circumstance.

#24. When and how should I set up bookkeeping for my new business?

As soon as you know you're going ahead with plans to start your business, bookkeeping should be one of your first projects. Accurate records are essential and make your life infinitely easier; they show if you are doing well and where you can improve, they help track seasonal patterns, and they tell you where you can afford to make changes. Plus, they are necessary in the event of an IRS audit.

Keep receipts of every penny you spend and receive. Create a clear paper trail. And do some research about bookkeeping methods and tips for small businesses and self-employed people. You can find good information at *www.allbusiness.com, www.onlineorganizing .com, www.sba.gov, www.score.org,* and *www.internetbasedmoms.org,* among other sites.

#25. What is a business plan, and what should mine include?

A business plan describes your business and goals to anyone who might be interested, including lenders. It will serve as the blueprint of your business, laying out whether you will have employees or work alone in your dining room, helping you anticipate and handle unforeseen snags and emergencies and make good decisions about growing your business.

If you think you might apply for a loan, a good business plan matters because the lender can see specific and organized information about you, your partners, and your ability to repay the money you borrow. It also can help enlighten your own partners and managers regarding your vision for the company.

You can keep it simple, but at the very minimum, your business plan should contain:

- Information about the owners, start-up plans, client potential, number and expertise of employees, and where and how the business will operate.
- List of products and services, including those you anticipate for the future.
- Suppliers and others who will support you in some way.
- Balance sheet and income projections.
- A three-year projection of profits, expenses, numbers regarding sales or clients, and anticipated problems.

#26.   What should I know if I'm opening a store online?

First, you must take stock of your competition. It's one thing to sell your magnificent roasted coffee in your cute shop in your quaint hometown. But anyone wanting to buy great roasted coffee online can travel virtually to La Selva Negra in Nicaragua, or Café Milagros in Costa Rica, and buy some of the finest coffee in the world. Why would they buy yours? If you can't answer that question with confidence, your online store won't do well.

Next, you need a compelling website that you update regularly. You probably will need to hire a designer and webmaster to keep the site fresh. Distribution will also be key; you must have a way to ship to your customers easily and quickly. It's also a good idea to give them several shipment options so they can get the item overnight.

Good customer service also matters—and since you will be selling to customers across the country (and possibly worldwide), you will need someone working the service phones far beyond your normal coffee shop hours. This can be one of those outsourcing opportunities we mentioned earlier. You will need a toll-free number and credit card options.

An online store isn't the most difficult thing in the world to set up, but it has its complexities and you shouldn't attempt to perform all of these functions alone. Talk to advisors, and do some online shopping yourself to pinpoint what you enjoy, what's valuable, and what you don't like about it. With online shopping, getting quality results conveniently and immediately are the way to succeed.

#27. **What are the major pros and cons of buying an existing business?**

Pros:

- Your risk is lower with an established business. You can see records of their cash flow, fiscal challenges, and seasonal patterns. You already have an opinion as to its current location. You can review relationships with suppliers and deals extended to current customers.
- If the business is profitable, the transition can be almost seamless; you can begin earning money from the start. If you chose wisely, you can bring in revenues above your loan payments and earn profits quickly.
- Buying a profitable business gives you a head start in profitability. You can manage it at its current level and invest more time and energy in boosting profits even more.

Cons:

- Your initial investment will be more than if you were starting a new business. Say you want to open an Italian restaurant. You can start small, opening a neighborhood place or pizza parlor, open for lunch only. But if you buy an existing, successful restaurant, you will pay top dollar for the restaurant and invest in more staff, space, decorating costs, liquor license, and other expenses.
- There might be reasons why the current owner is selling the business that you don't know about—reasons that could restrict your future profits. A safety issue or a flooding

problem could be developing, or former staff could have done something to affect the business's reputation.

- If the former owner was an icon in the area or in his industry, you might have to prove yourself to customers—a bit like starting from scratch, only more expensive. How can you compete with Guido's spaghetti sauce, once Guido moves on?

#28.   I'd like to buy an existing business. Where do I search for a good one?

There are a number of resources where you might find a healthy business to purchase. Your first step should be to talk about your plans with colleagues in the industry. For example, if you want to buy an accounting business, talk to some CPAs to see if they know other accountants planning to sell. If you want to buy an interior design firm, ask around the design community. Other search ideas include:

- Advertise in the local and regional newsletters of organizations for your targeted audience. Check the websites of those organizations, too, because they may have a page for classified ads.
- Check your local newspaper and business magazines under "Businesses for Sale" or "Business Opportunities."
- Talk with business brokers who specialize in that industry; they may be able to find a business for sale.
- Check online sites such as *www.bizbuysell.com* and *www .bizquest.com*.

#29. How do I research a company that interests me?

Any business that is up for sale will have its books open for you to examine, from profitability to problems. Be prepared to sign a confidentiality agreement, a document that says you will keep all aspects of the sale, and the business you are researching, confidential. You should have a CPA ready to help you look over the financial records, and an attorney who will review the contracts and keep you aware of any legalities you need to know.

#30. Can I approach business owners directly, to ask if they are interested in selling?

If a business owner has advertised his company for sale, then of course he wants to sell. But approaching an owner who has not indicated his willingness to sell can be tricky, and might very well offend him. He might think you are implying he hasn't been a good businessman, or that you want to buy up area businesses with the idea of gentrifying or changing the neighborhood.

If you are determined to make an offer on a business that is not for sale, think of a sensitive way to approach the owner, or engage the services of a broker experienced in buying and selling businesses in that field.

#31. Is there a formula to help determine a fair price for a business?

Yes, there are formal calculations for book value and fair market value of a business—but they are riddled with subtle shadings for special circumstances and what-ifs. Your best bet is to talk with other owners of similar businesses to get an idea of values and a fair offer. If you don't know other owners, talk with the professionals at SCORE and do some online research at sites such as *www.toolkit.com*.

The list of factors to consider when buying an existing business is lengthy. You would begin by examining, with an attorney, all legal documents—contracts, leases, tax returns for at least three years, balance sheets, debts, sales records, and a current credit report. All tangible assets and real property involved in the deal should be inspected. You should also look at organizational charts and employee records, and get familiar with any licenses, permits, and zoning requirements relating to the business. All of these examinations are part of "due diligence," and you'll find many online resources to help you organize due diligence for purchasing your business.

#32. What are some advantages and disadvantages of buying a franchise?

From burgers to bread making, one of every eight businesses in America is a franchise. That tells you a lot of entrepreneurs see big advantages in linking their prosperity to an established name.

Advantages include:

- Most franchises are easily recognized brands, and people find a comfort level in spending their money on a familiar product. Drive into any town, and the local McDonald's will be much busier than a family-owned diner, even though food at the diner might be scrumptious. Promoting your business will be easier because it already enjoys name recognition.
- Often, part of what you buy in a franchise is management expertise. From hiring staff to where and when to advertise, your personal learning curve will be much shorter with a franchise. You benefit greatly from those who came before you.
- You have about 3,000 brands from which to choose. In 2008, that was the approximate number of franchise brands in the United States, representing more than

376,000 separate businesses, many of which are available for less than $10,000 per franchise. You can explore the possibilities at sites such as *www.allbusiness.com* and *www.franchiseexpo.com*.
■ The business already exists; you merely step in and run it.

However, franchises aren't for everyone who wants to be self-employed. Among their disadvantages:

■ Your up-front investment could be substantial. Although many franchises are relatively inexpensive to purchase, the average price is about $150,000, before you spend any money on payroll and other immediate costs. You also will pay royalty costs, defined in the answer to Question #33, that can run up to 6 percent of your gross revenues.

■ In an economic slump, it could be difficult to borrow the money to buy a successful franchise. We should note, however, that some franchise companies do offer financing options to purchasers.

■ Buying and operating a franchise may not be your ideal self-employment vision. Some aspects of franchise operations follow strict guidelines from the parent companies. Franchise holders of a famous (and delicious) bread-making chain can only use the franchisor's recipes, for instance. Some franchisees embrace the idea that their business will have some pre-set structure, while others bristle at it.

#33.   What is a master franchise? A franchise fee? A franchise royalty?

A master franchise is a license issued by the owner of a company, product, or service, granting another party the permission to offer franchise licenses to others. Say I own a Benetton clothing franchise, and I believe that my city could support three more Benetton stores. The owners of Benetton might grant me a master franchise, allowing me (for a fee) to "sell" Benetton franchises to others, thereby expanding the chain on the owners' behalf.

A franchise fee is the fee you pay to operate a franchise branch of a company, and to earn profits from your operation. A franchise royalty is paid to the franchisor (e.g., Benetton) after you open your franchise, usually a percentage of sales on an ongoing basis. This royalty is for your right to continue running the franchise and is a source of profit for the franchisor.

#34. How can I know if my business would make a successful franchise?

From fast food to video rental, drugstores and florist shops, franchising has changed the small business landscape—but that doesn't mean every business can succeed as a franchise. A successful franchise should:

- Show steady growth.
- Be profitable, including a return on the invested capital and the manager's salary.
- Be adaptable to different kinds of communities across the country.
- Have established procedures and systems, such as employee handbooks, training, and accounting processes.
- Be easy to learn; prospective franchisees should be able to learn the business in a month.

You will need to observe audits and sign a number of legal documents if you buy a franchise, so begin by consulting an attorney and an accountant who have worked with franchise purchases before. Make sure you collect all available information from the franchisor, including financial statements, company officers and structure, and a list of all other franchise owners, before you enter into any agreements.

Three prominent websites will help you prepare for your talks:

- *www.ftc.gov/bcp/franchise/netfran.htm*. On this site, you will find the relevant federal franchise laws and regulations.
- *www.franchise1.com*. This is the website of *The Franchise Handbook*, a quarterly publication dedicated to keeping franchisees informed.
- *www.franchise.org*, website of the International Franchise Association.

#35. Do you have any tips to help my franchise succeed?

Feeding and caring for a successful franchise is a lot like grooming any other kind of business. It's always helpful to talk with experts—both in franchising and in your business field—to get their opinions before you hire attorneys to begin drawing up contracts. You need to be confident that your business idea will work as a franchise.

From there, a franchise is a business. People respond positively to quality products and great service, and if both of those elements are at the top of their range, customers will pay a competitive price.

Develop relationships, not one-time customers. You want to be the only dry cleaner on people's minds. Be efficient—keep track of how long it takes to accomplish something, and work to improve those numbers all the time. And hire staff who believe in your product and will tell you the truth about everything, including your own mistakes.

PART 2

The Office

IT'S A ROOM you either have fun designing and arranging, or don't give any thought to at all. You can just shove aside a few boxes and set up your laptop, right? Wrong. It's amazing how deeply our surroundings affect us. When your office is neatly organized, with your files filed and plenty of uncluttered desk space, you are likely to focus better and work more efficiently. But when the floor is so littered with magazine piles that you have to step over them in order to reach your desk, and the desktop is covered with several layers of scribbled notes-to-self, you won't accomplish nearly as much.

Privacy, too, is central to a home office design. You may be looking forward to more time with the kids and Fido when you work from home and, indeed, flexibility in your workday is one of the all-time wonderful perks of being self-employed at home. But when you're working, you need to be working—in a quiet, dedicated workspace, free of intrusion from family and friends.

This section will help you set up your office for efficient workflow, and guide you through the perils and advantages of doing business at home. (You'll also read more about these issues in Part 5, when we discuss time, privacy, and other work-at-home considerations.)

Here you will gain insight on office layout, selecting furniture and equipment, and how much you should plan to spend. Image may or may not be a factor, but productivity is key.

#36.   **Do I need major office equipment—printer, copier, fax, postage meter—for my home office?**

Beyond your computer, your "major" equipment isn't as major as it used to be. Even your computer doesn't have to take up much desk space. Most businesses operating from a home office can get by with a laptop, and you can find fairly souped-up models for $1,200 or less. Designers need to spend more for software and larger screens, but for all industries, flat-screen personal computers (PCs) or Macs give a sleek, space-efficient look to an office.

For printers and copiers, you can buy a sophisticated name-brand, all-in-one (printer, scanner, copier, and fax) for about $150. Stand-alone fax machines are redundant and outdated; don't bother buying one. And unless you're sending bulk mailings, you probably don't need a postage meter, as most print communications now happen online. Postage should be a minor expense in your new business.

#37.   **I'm not a techie. How do I choose a computer for my new small business?**

Your first decision is, PC/Windows or Macintosh? If you haven't sat down to work at both systems, ask a friend if you can use theirs for a short time. You'll need to choose which will serve your company's needs better.

Consider the computer's memory, or storage capacity. At a minimum, get at least 2G (2 gigs) of memory, and ask if the computer that interests you can be upgraded. You'll also need a DVD burner for easier data back-up, and at least two data ports (USB connections) to connect to printers, cameras, and other devices.

Beyond those most basic considerations, ask other small business owners what they find handy in terms of both hardware and software. They can suggest their favorite bookkeeping and time management software, and computer features they can't live without.

#38. What are the pros and cons of purchasing reconditioned computers and other office equipment?

The biggest advantage, obviously, is the cost. I once bought an IBM ThinkPad, probably a $2,400 machine at the time, for $700 from an online "seconds" website. It was a good machine, lightweight and versatile, but its memory was diminished. It became sluggish after about six months, and none of the normal remedies worked. In the two years I worked with that laptop, I had two crises that put it in the repair shop for a week each time. IBM's customer service people were wonderful, but I had bought an old, outdated machine. I finally gave it to a niece and bought myself a new laptop.

Remember, old laptops come with built-in risks. For your new business, buy a new model with plenty of software and easy access to the manufacturer's tech support, which can be a lifesaver to a non-techie.

#39. What are the pros and cons of leasing, rather than purchasing, office equipment?

In this decision, too, your biggest deciding factor will be the cost. Leasing equipment enables you to spend less on your initial investment and build the business before you make some major purchases. Your payments will be tax deductible and, if the equipment becomes outdated, you can lease a newer model when the lease expires.

For a home office, however, your cost for office equipment may not justify leasing. Even if you need a very elaborate computer system—say, one that costs $5,000—your payments over a three-year lease probably would cost about $9,000. You won't build equity, and if you don't like the equipment, you're stuck with it for a long time.

Buying does give you ownership benefits, tax deductions, and the possibility of a tax deduction for depreciation. But your initial cost will be higher, and you may have to replace the equipment after a few years.

#40. **What is the most efficient way to arrange my office?**

One of the biggest mistakes in arranging a home office is making too much horizontal space. It's tempting to purchase a huge work table that stretches along one wall—but inevitably, it quickly fills with papers and you still won't have a place for things you need. Better to go with a desk system that flows up the wall, so you can reach for reference books, calculators and other smaller items that can get buried under messy paper piles.

Keep those things near you that you'll need all the time. If you print every day, position your printer where you can reach it from your desk chair. Storage can be in the closet, with supplies stacked neatly on floor-to-ceiling shelves—no need to keep reams of paper or boxes of file folders out in the open. But do keep supplies handy that you use; if you print often, keep a stash of paper at the printer.

The goal in arranging an office is to eliminate the need to get up and walk around every time you need a dictionary, an envelope, a rubber band. Think about how you work and what you use all the time, and let form follow function.

#41. **My office is being overrun with documents. How do I avoid the inevitable reams of records?**

There's no need to bury yourself under a mountain of paper. Buy a reliable scanner and scan all possible documents. If you own a medical practice for example, electronic records are better for patients, who can request them from anywhere in the world if they experience a medical emergency or if another doctor wants to complete his or her medical profile of the individual. Electronic records are also better for the planet because, ultimately, you'll use less paper, thereby creating less trash. And you'll be happier in your home office if you aren't dealing with dusty boxes of records.

One paper document you must keep, however, is your federal income tax return. Depending on your circumstances, the U.S. Internal Revenue Service (IRS) wants you to keep your return for up to seven years. I hang onto mine for about ten years—but don't clutter your office with those old papers. Put them in storage.

#42.   **I've set up my home office, but frankly, it's a depressing space. Any tips for transforming it into a place I'll enjoy and can be productive every day?**

First, look at the location. I've always thought basements were depressing under the best circumstances; I can't imagine being motivated down there. If you're beneath ground level, find a way to climb up into the land of the living. If you don't have a spare room above-ground, consider renting a small office in a city neighborhood, where rents usually are affordable.

A few more tips:

- Lighten up! If you're surrounded by dark paneling, paint it white, or perhaps a soft yellow. Place strong task lighting at your work spaces, and be sure to create a comfortable spot where you can read—with a good reading lamp.
- Use cheerful accessories. Even a man-cave can use a spark of color in a pillow or wall art. Let the room welcome you each day, with your favorite paintings or artifacts from your travels.
- "Spark" some fresh energy in your new office with a candle, a chime on the door, or an aromatherapy diffuser. Don't use a heavy scent; keep it light and pleasant so you won't be distracted as you're working.

#43. I want to "go green" with my business. How can my office reflect my concern for the environment?

Entire books have been written about creating a green office, so you have plenty of resources. The Sierra Club (*www.sierraclub.org*) offers ten tips to get you started:

1. Turn off the lights when you leave a room, and use only Energy-Star–rated light bulbs, which use up to two-thirds less electricity.
2. Turn off your computer at the end of the day, and put it to sleep during the workday when it's not being used.
3. Office workers in this country each use an average of 10,000 sheets of copy paper a year! Start printing on both sides, and print on the back sides of old documents you no longer need. Recycle toner and ink cartridges.
4. Stop printing so much! Send and store documents online instead.
5. Recycle everything possible—paper, junk mail, cell phones, PDAs, pagers.
6. Only purchase office supplies made from recycled materials.
7. Eat and drink from reusable dishes, mugs, glasses and flatware—no paper plates. Consume organic coffee, tea, and food that was grown locally, and drink filtered tap water instead of bottled.
8. When you run errands or attend meetings, use public transportation whenever possible.
9. If you must drive, try to purchase a hybrid car. Other alternative transportation includes bicycling, carpooling, and walking.
10. Use nontoxic cleaning products and paints, and improve the air quality in your office with houseplants.

#44. **Where can I find decent office furniture without spending too much money?**

You don't have to go far to find sturdy, attractive, functional office furniture. Office supply stores in your city, including the big chains, have frequent sales. Discount furnishers such as IKEA (*www.ikea.com*) offer wide selections of desk systems, chairs, filing cabinets, shelving, and other office needs. Still others sell "seconds"—furniture that is new but may have a scratch or other minor flaw that you can easily camouflage.

Pay attention to the shipping terms. At IKEA, for instance, you can find inexpensive furniture but in most instances, you will assemble it yourself—and if you can't pick it up at a nearby store, you'll pay premium shipping costs. Other stores might deliver already-assembled furniture free of charge. It pays to shop around; shipping costs for heavy furniture can add $150 or more to your total price.

#45. **How do I find discounts on office supplies?**

Some good options for finding less expensive office supplies include:

- Look for coupons in daily mailers, your Sunday newspaper, and at office supply stores.
- Buy in bulk. You can pay the same price for a package of three pens that you would pay for a box of twelve, and purchasing copy paper by the box can save you up to $20 each time you buy. From paper towels to printer ink cartridges, you almost always will save money by buying in bulk.
- Buy supplies through your trade association. You can easily save enough money by using the association's group discount to cover your annual dues. If your association doesn't

yet offer group discounts on office supplies, ask the executive director to make the necessary calls. The big-box office supply stores maintain such relationships with groups across the country.

#46. What are some easy techniques for organizing files and paperwork?

For starters, organize online whenever possible—create folders for your documents, then send files to a large site such as *www .gmail.com* for storage. Back everything up on an external flash drive and a CD.

For office paperwork, a good rule is to touch it once—period. If it's a bill, pay it that day. If you need to keep it, file it now. If you don't need it, shred it.

Color coding can help organize files, either with colored tabs or file folders. Red might mean "Must Address This Week," green could mean, "New Ideas," and yellow could signify, "Not Urgent." Figure out half a dozen general categories that signify how and when something should be handled, and create files to match.

#47. I keep a lot of newsletters and magazines for reference. How can I cut down on that clutter?

First, do you really have to keep so many newsletters and magazines—or could you get away with one or two examples of each, and clip an occasional article from other issues?

If you haven't referred to a magazine or newsletter in the past six months, shred it. In the unlikely event that you do need any of that information, it will be outdated. It might be archived online, or you can clip articles that interest you and keep them in one of those color-coded files.

#48. **What is the ideal space for a home-based office?**

The main feature of your home office should be a door that closes. You need an office where you can work without interruption or excessive noise and where you can take phone calls from clients and focus on the job at hand, without being disturbed by children or pets. This privacy issue can be a major challenge for newly self-employed people. If your family has trouble accepting that you're "at work" when you're in the office, set firm boundaries and hold a family meeting to let them know that you need your privacy.

You're going to spend a lot of time in your home office, so make it a comfortable place. A damp basement or sweltering attic won't work; if the room itself is unpleasant, you won't want to go in there. Give it good ventilation and temperature control, and have some fun with the space. A fresh coat of paint will change the tone. Bring in some art, awards you've won, and music if it helps you relax. I don't recommend a television in the office; you don't want to relax so much in there that you stop working.

#49. **I don't have an actual spare room for my new home-based business. How can I create a dedicated workplace in another room?**

It's not easy to earn a living amidst the bustle of a noisy family, but it can be done. What's most important is that you have a work-only space—even if it's just the corner of your dining room—where kids or roommates will respect your privacy. If there's space, set up a folding screen to help give you more privacy and a business-cubicle feeling. Buy good earphones if you'll be coping with distracting noise while you work, and set up your own computer and phone. Network your computer to others in the house so you can send documents to a printer in another room.

However, if the corner of your dining room is the best office space you can carve out at home, consider renting an office outside your home. You will be more productive, and your house will be less cluttered. Office space can be more affordable than you might think; look into neighborhood venues (as opposed to pricey office space in the center city). Or, talk to other self-employed acquaintances about leasing a space together to keep costs down for all of you.

#50. Clients will be visiting my office. How can I give it a professional appearance?

View your office as part of your outward appearance, and remember that you only have one chance to make a good first impression. Clean and businesslike are the key words—no kids' toys strewn about the room, and no piles of newspapers on the floor.

It's acceptable to place your office in a non-glamorous setting; many offices of highly successful companies are located in warehouses. But only Tony Soprano can get away with working out of a strip joint, and you need to give your office a sophisticated look even if it's not elegant. Sit at a "real" desk—no card tables, please!—and invest in sturdy, comfortable chairs. If you've earned degrees or certificates, hang them on the wall, along with some tasteful artwork. That could mean a framed pair of antique lace gloves, an autographed photo of Mickey Mantle or a pretty plate. It doesn't have to be expensive, just tasteful. And keep your desk clean.

#51. I manage with my office in the dining room, but I need to meet with clients from time to time. Any ideas?

It's perfectly fine to meet with a client over coffee, breakfast, or lunch. Choose a place that's affordable enough that you won't panic if you offer to pick up the tab and the client accepts. There may be times when you'll need a small conference room; for those occasions, consider renting a meeting space. One good example of such places is SparkSpace *(www.sparkspace.com)* in Columbus, Ohio, a restored warehouse where clients can meet and, if they choose, have a healthy buffet breakfast or lunch brought in.

#52. I've heard of home offices being shut down for zoning violations. How do I avoid such a catastrophe?

Go to your town's municipal building or City Hall and ask to speak with a zoning official about restrictions for your type of business. Many residents feel strongly that they want to keep neighborhood traffic to a minimum, so checking these codes in advance could prevent an expensive mistake down the road.

#53. I'll have a part-time assistant for my home-based business. How can I find a space for her in my very small office?

Consider hiring a virtual assistant (VA) instead—an assistant who does most of her work off-site. VAs can do billing, customer service, bookkeeping, write your blog, answer e-mails, maintain your website, compose correspondence, run errands, and most other tasks that an in-office assistant would perform. Hiring a VA takes the pressure off of you to keep her busy during prescribed hours, and gives you more privacy. You can assign her whatever tasks you choose and meet with her regularly.

#54. Could I find a VA to do more technical work?

You could find a VA to do almost anything. The 1,000-plus members of the International Virtual Assistants Organization (IVAA) are independent entrepreneurs offering creative, administrative, and technical services, and they include accountants, marketers, editors, graphic designers, paralegals, transcribers, and translators. For information, go to *www.ivaa.org*.

#55. Is taking a home-office deduction on my income taxes a "red flag" to Internal Revenue Service auditors?

According to accountants consulted for this book, no—your chances of being audited by the IRS are no higher with a home office deduction than without one. If you make sure that (a) your home office deduction is within the range the IRS would say is "reasonable" for your profession, your income, and your home; and (b) you truly have a home office. In most years, that means a space dedicated exclusively to earning a living, with no other activities in that room. I wouldn't bank on that corner in the dining room being accepted by a tax auditor.

I say "in most years" because the IRS tax rules are complicated; what's acceptable changes every year and often is open to interpretation. The IRS recommends that all taxpayers take every deduction due them—but if you have any doubt regarding your deductions, consult a CPA.

PART 3

Financial and Legal Aspects

IF THIS IS your first self-employment adventure, the financial and legal issues can be intimidating. From here on, you will have no employer to handle your paycheck and withdrawals such as federal, state, and municipal income taxes, Social Security tax, and health insurance. Billing and collecting from clients will be your responsibility now. You will handle the financial records (or oversee the person doing that job) and make sure the business doesn't cross any legal, ethical, or moral lines. The concept of accepting ultimate responsibility for nearly everything that happens in your business can be overwhelming.

The good news is if you do your research and lay the right groundwork, the financials and legalities of a business really are straightforward and logical. Your best chance at success is to get guidance and advice from the beginning. Don't venture into any fiscal or legal areas that confuse you, or for which you are unprepared or unqualified. From your banker to the volunteers at SCORE, you have many resources that can help answer questions and show you how to get from one point to the next. Use them.

#56.   **What does my personal credit score have to do with being self-employed?**

A couple of developments in your financial snapshot are inevitable when you begin to work for yourself. The first is that you probably will use credit differently. At the beginning, most self-employed people acquire large balances on their credit cards because there's a lot of shopping involved, and they don't want to spend all of their cash. Those higher balances could lower your credit score.

You also will start taking income tax deductions for your business expenses. These new deductions will, in the eyes of the IRS, lower your income considerably. So if your income decreases and your credit score is lower, how will a lender respond if you need to buy a new car or refinance your house? That's the connection between your credit score and self-employment.

Before you start working for yourself, talk to your financial advisor about how you can avoid problems with your credit score during your first few years of self-employment. If you see any major borrowing on the horizon, you may want to apply for that loan before you leave your current job.

#57.   **How do I learn my credit score and credit history?**

The story of your credit score really lies in your credit report. Under the Fair Credit Reporting Act, consumers can obtain three free credit reports per year. Only one website can provide it: *www .annualcreditreport.com*. When you go to the site, click on your state and fill out the required forms. You will be asked which of the three credit reporting agencies you want to send you a form; consider using your three-report quota for requesting one report from each agency. There may be differences between them; if your score isn't as high as you like, you will have all the data in front of you.

To obtain your accurate credit score, go to *www.myfico.com* and download the request form.

#58.   **What is the best way to establish credit for my new business?**

Before you can establish a new line of credit for your business, you probably will be asked to personally guarantee any business debts. So, the best way to establish new business credit is to have solid personal credit. Unless your own credit is good, a lender won't want to give you a business loan.

There are several ways to boost your credit score:

- **Check your credit reports to make sure they're accurate.** More than 8.3 million people are victims of identity theft each year. It's always possible that someone opened an account in your name, then didn't make payments on the account.
- **Never miss a payment.** Late or missed payments can account for up to one-third of your credit score.
- **Call your creditor immediately if you have a problem paying a bill on time.** Lenders often will make a one-time adjustment and "forgive" your lateness, just this once.
- **Pay down your balances.** Your debt-to-credit limit ratio accounts for another one-third of your credit score, so try not to let your balances exceed 50 percent of your credit limits.
- **Don't close any credit accounts.** The more open credit you have, the lower your debt-to-credit limit ratio. Keep your old accounts open, even if you don't need them.
- **Don't apply for new credit more often than you need it.** Bustling application activity sends a red flag to creditors, who might think you're having money troubles.

#59. **Should I have separate bank accounts and credit cards for my business?**

A business credit card keeps your business purchases separate from the sneakers and wine you might buy with your personal credit card. When income tax time comes around, it's easier to document your expenses if they all appear on one credit card statement and aren't mingled with personal purchases. If you don't want to apply for a business credit card, it's not required, but you do have to keep accurate records of expenses in order to claim them as business deductions from your income tax.

It also is not required to use separate business and personal bank accounts, though it makes for tidier bookkeeping. However, as one example, if you are a sole proprietor working from a home office, you probably will take a home office deduction, which would be a portion of your rent or mortgage payment. Which checking account would you use for paying the rent—personal or business?

If your business is very small, such as freelance graphic design, you don't need separate bank accounts—go ahead and pay rent and other business costs from your personal checking account—but do keep accurate records for business expenses.

#60. **Where can I get a grant to start my business?**

Although the federal government doesn't give grants to small businesses, many state development offices do. That should be the first stop in your search.

Thousands of private foundations, corporations, and organizations bestow grants on new and developing small businesses. Spend a little time searching online—simply Google "small business grants, (your profession)." You are sure to find plenty of grant sources, provided you meet their requirements.

#61. **Do I need to draw up contracts for the services I provide to my clients?**

Yes, you should provide a contract every time you provide a service to a client—but it doesn't need to be an elaborate or complicated document. It can be a one-page document, sent by e-mail, listing your expectations of each other—the work you will perform, your timeline, and how and when you expect to be compensated. I've provided a sample contract in Appendix A; feel free to use it as a model for your own Agreements with clients.

Such agreement letters boost your professional image. They also provide legal protection to both parties in case the job is not completed, or if payment isn't made.

#62. **Should I use bookkeeping software? How do I choose the right one?**

Even sole proprietors with simple expense and income records often use bookkeeping software now, just because it simplifies their recordkeeping. Such software makes it easy for you to sort and track expenses in different categories, rather than deal with a mountain of receipts when you're paying taxes.

If more than one person is involved in your business, then computerized records are essential, and software such as Quicken and Quikbooks will be helpful. Talk with others in businesses similar to yours and ask which software they use, because some software is better suited to certain businesses than to others. Most software manufacturers will allow you to use their products for a trial period.

#63. **Is there a formula for estimating my projected business expenses?**

There is no formula. The cost of opening and running a deli in one neighborhood will be vastly different from its counterpart across town, depending on their leases, size, number of employees, where they buy their salami, and dozens of other factors.

Two strategies will help you estimate your future expenses. One is to talk to those other deli owners; they can point you to the best salami providers, help you anticipate customer flow, and build a foundation for mutual support in the future. You will benefit by thinking of them as colleagues, rather than competitors.

The other aid will be a detailed business plan. You can find templates and guidebooks for writing business plans that are general and applicable to almost any small business, or that apply specifically to your business area. Don't overlook the IRS, who provides audit guides for many types of businesses. Their guide for bed-and-breakfasts, for instance, contains information on the average cost an innkeeper spends on food for each guest. Search online and in bookstores, use those resources, then write a business plan that's as detailed as possible.

#64. What kind of insurance coverage do I need for a home-based business?

You need to protect your life, health, and property, just as when you were an employee. You must insure yourself to safeguard your family's future. You should provide health insurance—not only for yourself, but for any employees, because providing good benefits will enable you to recruit and retain a good staff. It's also a good idea to provide life insurance for employees; that protection is relatively inexpensive. And you need property insurance to protect against theft or natural disaster.

#65. Does my homeowner's insurance cover my home-based business?

Your homeowner's insurance covers your home and furnishings, regardless of whether they are used for work or leisure. However, it's a good idea to review your coverage occasionally, especially when you start a new business. If you've purchased a new computer system or furnishings for your office, it might make sense to increase your coverage. Also, your policy may have clauses that affect coverage of an employee or intern who spends a lot of time in your home, as well as liability regarding clients who visit you. Ask your representative to review your policy.

#66. **What's my personal liability as a sole proprietor, and what protection do I need?**

Depending on the corporate structure of your business—i.e., whether you are incorporated, and if so, what kind of corporation you've formed—you can encounter a variety of liability issues. One that should be covered by homeowner's insurance is general liability, covering personal injuries to individuals visiting your property.

Your homeowner's insurance will not protect you, however, in the event that you are sued for libel, slander, and offenses such as malpractice. Such liability issues are complex, and insurance for them can be an exorbitant cost. It's a necessary expense in some types of businesses, such as a medical or dental practice, but if you're using your telephone for freelance customer service work you won't need this type of coverage. Talk to your attorney and insurance agent; they'll know where you are vulnerable and how much coverage you need.

#67. **What insurance do I need for a small business not based at home—say, an auto repair shop or coffee shop?**

You need to insure the buildings and furnishings, though if you're leasing the space, the building itself should be insured by the owner. Furnishings, including desks, chairs, and equipment, might be referred to as "business personal property." You also will need fire legal liability to protect you and your business if a fire starts because of your faulty equipment or carelessness, general liability insurance for your space in case someone is injured tripping over a rug in your office, and worker's compensation insurance, required by law if you have employees. If you have a company car, auto insurance is legally required; check with your state's motor vehicle department for the exact requirements in your state.

It's not mandatory to provide health insurance for employees, but it's the number-one benefit on every job hunter's mind, and it will give you an edge when you try to recruit good staff. And if your business makes or repairs products, you may need separate coverage to insure the safety of the products and health insurance for employees. General liability insurance for customers is required by law, as is worker's compensation insurance if you have employees. You also need auto insurance for company vehicles.

#68. **Where can I find affordable health insurance as a self-employed person?**

While "affordable health insurance" is one of my least favorite oxymorons, the landscape is changing. Health care reform legislation aims to ease the burden of this country's millions of uninsured persons.

If you need private health insurance and belong to a trade association, check to see if the organization offers group health insurance to its members. If not, talk to your colleagues in the same industry and learn your options. Check, too, with other large organizations to which you belong, such as AARP (the American Association of Retired Persons), then shop around for the best coverage you can afford. Many websites, such as *www.einsurance.com*, display apples-to-apples figures on the site and will give you an individualized quote.

#69.   **What is a Health Savings Account (HSA)?**

An HSA is an account where you deposit money to pay for future health care—a savings account with a specific purpose. You control the deposits and withdrawals; you don't have to ask an insurance company whether you can spend those funds for certain treatments. You must be enrolled in a high-deductible health plan in order to open an HSA; theoretically such a plan costs significantly less than coverage with a low deductible, and participants deposit the money saved in their HSA. You can open an HSA at any bank or credit union.

#70.   **What's the difference between tangible, intangible, and intellectual property?**

Tangible property is anything that can be touched—your building, desk, computer, etc. Intangible property is something you own and can transfer to another person, but has no physical substance, such as patents, trademarks, and copyrights. Exceptions to the tangible/intangible definition are items you can touch, but which represent intangible things, such as a promissory note. For example, an I.O.U. usually is a piece of paper that you can touch, but it represents a debt, which isn't something you can hold in your hand.

Intellectual property is the legal property right over creations of the mind, including literary and artistic works, paintings, photos, software, and the designs of "knock-off" handbags.

#71.   **How can I protect my intellectual property?**

If your intellectual property is an invention, you will want a patent on it—a complicated process for which you may want to consult an attorney. A copyright protects original works of authorship, including literary, musical, and dramatic works, plus software, and audio and visual recordings. As soon as the work is "fixed in a tangible medium," such as published in a book, copyright protection is in effect. Copyright differs from trademark protection, which prevents other businesses from selling a product under the same name. Only Kimberly-Clark can sell Kleenex, though other companies can produce and sell their own facial tissues.

#72. Define a "sole proprietorship." How do I know that's the best business structure for me?

A sole proprietorship is a business that is not incorporated. It's the simplest business structure for a number of reasons: Incorporation is a legal term that means, literally, the process of creating a corporation. Such businesses must file documents with the state in which the corporation is located; those documents, called "Articles of Incorporation," officially state what the corporation does, and who is involved as officers of the company. All funds and liabilities of the company are kept separate from your personal money and obligations.

Incorporating is a complicated matter. A sole proprietor, on the other hand, simply pays the bills for the business, including taxes, out of his or her personal income. The debts of the business are the individual's debts, and business expenses are listed as income tax deductions. It's a straightforward system, easy for almost any solo entrepreneur to manage.

#73. I'm a sole proprietor—when should I consider incorporating?

Maybe you shouldn't. If your business is the kind that often incurs liability and is targeted for lawsuits, such as a medical practice, then you should incorporate to protect your personal assets from lawsuits and creditors. Incorporation also is an answer for people who don't want their business income treated as personal income for some reason, or have it included on their personal tax return.

However, for some self-employed people, incorporating can present big disadvantages:

- It's a costly move. Depending on your state's regulations and type of business, the initial fees to incorporate can be significant. There also can be ongoing fees to maintain your corporate status.
- The time and cost involved with the record-keeping required of corporations can overwhelm a sole proprietor.
- Watch out for the frustrations of double taxation. The profits of your incorporated business will be taxed, as well as your personal dividends or income.
- Once your business is incorporated, its funds must be kept totally separate from your personal money. That means separate bank accounts and no "borrowing" if you're a little low on cash.

Most sole proprietors with five-figure incomes see no need to incorporate, but if you think it might hold advantages for you, consult your accountant.

#74.   **What does it take to incorporate?**

You can incorporate by filling out forms online and paying several hundred dollars, but check with an attorney first to learn both the requirements in your state and the ramifications. If you incorporate, you cannot mingle personal funds with the business's money; you must have separate accounts. It's also necessary to keep records a certain way and to hold regular meetings. Incorporating is a big step and a lot of work, so get professional guidance.

#75.   **What is an S corporation? What are the advantages of becoming one?**

An S corporation has shareholders but is taxed like a sole proprietorship; its shareholders report business income or losses on their personal tax returns. An S corporation has to file a tax return but as an entity does not pay the taxes. As with other types of corporations, the S-corp designation does offer some liability protection to shareholders, plus their Social Security tax obligations are diminished. However, it can be expensive to set up, and the regulations can be a burden. Plus, the IRS often targets S corporations for audits.

#76.   **What's the difference between a limited partnership and a general partnership?**

In a business partnership, or general partnership, two or more people who are not married own a business together. There are no documents to file, and all partners share equal authority in running the business. They are liable for its debts, including debts to other partners. So, if you are one of four partners and one of them borrows $5,000 from you for a computer system and can't repay it, the remaining two partners are liable for that debt.

A limited partnership requires a formal, written agreement among partners, and you must file some papers with the State. There are limits on partners' liability; they can only lose as much as they invested. However, they don't have as much individual control over the company; partners must choose at least one general partner who controls day-to-day operations and can make legally binding decisions. Unlike the other partners, general partners are personally liable for the company's debts.

While the popular image of a self-employed person is the sole proprietor working alone, I wanted to include these brief notes about a limited partnership because individuals often do "partner up" to start a business. If they're not employees of someone else's company, I think of these partners-in-ownership as self-employed people: they started their business and they own it.

#77. Are a limited partnership and a limited liability company (LLC) the same thing?

No, an LLC is much like a partnership but it has members instead of partners. Most states permit single-member LLCs, which are taxed like sole proprietorships. If the LLC has two or more members, it's taxed as a partnership.

#78. What if I start a partnership and later decide I can't work with my partners?

There are a number of formal, legal ways to end all business partnerships. Your attorney can inform you of the options in your state.

#79. What are business incubators?

A business incubator is a place where small-business owners can share support and advice for their new businesses. Incubators can be sponsored by universities, foundations, or organizations that form just for that purpose. They can be informal gatherings or companies in themselves, such as Ladies Who Launch, a national network of women entrepreneurs that began in 2002 as an online e-mail group.

#80. Do I need an operating license for my home-based business?

Most cities or counties require some type of business license. Sole proprietors working from home offices were once exempt from licensing, but cities are increasingly requiring them to be licensed as well. Call your town hall to ask if you need a local business license. If your business provides services that are regulated by state law, such as those provided by private investigators or hairstylists, you will need a state license as well. Retail businesses also must have a sales tax license.

Some occupations also require permits—a seller's permit, building permit, health permit (if you're preparing food), zoning permit, or home occupation permit, among other types. Or you may need no permits at all. Check with others in your town who work in the same business, or call the appropriate agency. Failure to obtain the proper permit, if one is required, could bring fines or a shutdown by the authorities.

#81. Will I need a vendor's license for my new business?

Here, too, the regulations depend on where you live. Generally, any business that collects and pays sales tax to the State needs a vendor's license in the county in which the sales are made. All retail sellers need a vendor's license. Contact your State Department of Taxation to find out whether you qualify and how to apply.

#82. How do I register (or otherwise protect) the name of my new business?

If you are a sole proprietor, your full name is the legal name of your business. If it's a partnership, its name is the one specified in your partnership agreement, or the partners' last names. And if your business is a corporation or LLC, its name is the one you registered with the state government.

The legal name of your business should appear on all forms, licenses, and permits. Or, you could choose a "fictitious name," such as Nutty Muffin Shop or Fast Sneakers. That name should be registered with the state or county, depending on your area's laws.

#83.   How should I handle billing my clients?

Experts suggest that the more quickly and accurately you record your billable hours, the less reason you'll give clients to dispute an invoice. You should follow a regular billing schedule—every week or two weeks—so your cash flow won't suffer. And it's amazing how promptly people pay when you offer them an incentive; giving customers a 2 percent discount if they pay within 14 days is sure to boost your on-time payments.

#84.   What steps should I take if payment is overdue?

If this is a long-term client whom you believe will be a good customer again, go to him. Let him propose a payment plan; try to keep the relationship. Often, customers pay late either because the invoice was delayed, or the company made an error, such as sending your payment to the wrong address. But if the payment truly is late, don't be complacent. Talk with the individual in charge, find out if there's a problem, and deal with it. The solution could be as simple as adjusting the payment schedule for certain clients.

If that doesn't work, distance yourself from the customer. Let someone else talk to him, possibly a collection agency, and don't do any more business with the person until you're paid in full. You don't want to get into a deeper hole yourself. With longtime customers, aggressive action, such as a collection agency, should be a last resort—but if the customer is in financial trouble, do take action to ensure that you will be among the creditors who get paid.

#85.   Should I sue a nonpaying client in Small Claims Court?

Suing someone in Small Claims Court is an effective remedy if their debt to you is under a specified amount, which differs from state to state. You don't need an attorney. In order to use Small Claims Court, either you or the party you're suing must reside or do business in that court's jurisdiction—so if you're based in Des Moines and the delinquent customer is in Miami, you must sue either in the Des Moines court, which wouldn't have much effect on a Miami deadbeat, or the Miami court. In the latter case, you would need someone there on the court date to represent you—possibly not worth the trouble if the court's limit is $2,000 to $5,000.

#86. What do "business cash flow" and "net after-tax income" mean?

Business cash flow is the money coming into and going out of a business. You pay for supplies, facilities, or people's time, and you collect money when you sell other goods and services. Cash is king; without cash flow you have no business.

Net after-tax income is the same as net cash flow—your after-tax income or loss, otherwise known as your true bottom line, when there's nothing else to add or subtract.

#87. What are gross profit and net profit?

Gross profit is your revenue before you deduct the cost of making a product or providing a service. To figure your net profit, you subtract all of your expenses—overhead, personnel costs, taxes—and you are left with the net profit, or the bottom line.

#88. I don't know anything about accounting, but I don't want that to stop me from launching my business. Where can I find a simple tutorial?

You will find a wealth of beginner's accounting information online, starting with the Small Business Administration's website. Go to *www.sba.gov,* click on "Free Online Training," and see courses from Intro to Accounting to Technology 101, Exporting, and Franchising. Also check out these free instructional sites: *www.payroll.intuit.com, www.wannalearn.com,* and *www.dwmbeancounter.com.* You'll find thousands more to explore by searching at *www.google.com.*

#89. I'm a sole proprietor. Should I use a Federal ID number or Individual Taxpayer Identification Number (ITIN) in the business, instead of my Social Security number?

In order to pay your self-employment tax, you must have either a Social Security number or an ITIN. If you cannot get a Social Security number for some reason (for instance, if you are not a U.S. citizen), then the IRS will issue you an ITIN if you apply with Form W-7. Otherwise, you should use your Social Security number.

#90. What does it mean to "certify" my business, and what are the advantages?

Certified businesses have applied for and received a government designation that allows them certain privileges in competing for work. Businesses owned by women, veterans, minorities, and homosexuals often are certified—it is a credential they can use in attracting government jobs—and organizations whose members match those categories lend their support to those businesses. Certified businesses also use the credential in marketing and promoting themselves; it makes them a very attractive provider to certain clients.

#91. When does the IRS consider me self-employed?

The IRS says you are self-employed if any of these apply to you:

- You carry on a trade or business as a sole proprietor or an independent contractor.
- You are a member of a partnership that carries on a trade or business.
- You are otherwise in business for yourself.

#92. What is self-employment tax?

Self-employment tax is a Social Security and Medicare tax for individuals who work for themselves. It's paid to the IRS and is a pay-as-you-go tax. The IRS expects self-employed people to pay it on a quarterly basis, in advance of each quarter of the calendar year. (Due dates on the payments, however, are slightly off-kilter: April 15, June 15, September 15, and January 15.)

#93. Who must pay self-employment tax?

You must pay self-employment tax and file Schedule SE (Form 1040) if your earnings from self-employment were $400 or more for the year, or if you had church employee income of $108.28. These tax rules apply regardless of your age, even if you already are receiving Social Security or Medicare.

Once you become self-employed, the IRS should send you payment coupons to accompany each check during the year. If you earn more than the wages covered in advance by your quarterly payments, you will have to pay additional taxes by April 15 of the following year, just as all taxpayers must pay.

#94. Do self-employed people have to pay federal income tax, Medicare tax, and/or unemployment tax?

Yes, self-employed people must pay federal income tax. Their Medicare tax is part of their self-employment tax (as is their

Social Security contribution); they don't have to pay it separately. And no, self-employed people do not pay unemployment tax.

#95. **What is a W-2 form and do sole proprietors need one?**

Form W-2 is the form that employers distribute to their employees and to the IRS at year's end, showing the employee's earnings and the amounts withheld for taxes. No, sole proprietors do not need a W-2 unless they also collected "W-2 income" during the year as an employee.

#96. **What is a 1099 form and would a self-employed person need one?**

Form 1099-MISC shows the income earned from a client, but there are no funds withheld for federal, state, or municipal income taxes, nor for Social Security or other withholdings. While employers generally withhold those items from their employees' paychecks, self-employed individuals are responsible for making those payments themselves.

Any person or company that pays you more than $600 during the year for your services must send you a 1099-MISC by January 30 of the following year. However, as a sole proprietor, you must report to the IRS—and pay taxes on—all of your income, not just that from higher-paying clients. If you earned $125 writing a neighbor's resume, that amount should be reported when you file your income tax.

#97. **What are asset depreciation and amortization?**

Asset depreciation refers to the decline in value of an asset, such as a computer, over its lifetime because of age, normal wear and tear, or because it has become obsolete.

Amortization takes a different view; it refers to an asset's decline in value by prorating its cost—and, therefore, your income tax deduction for that item—over a number of years.

#98. **What are some typical home-office deductions?**

Home-office deductions include costs for that space (rent, heat, electricity, water), equipment (computer, printer), furnishings (desk, chair, shelves, cupboards, storage bins, lamps), office supplies, postage, reference materials, telephone and Internet connections, and other costs pertaining to doing business in that spot. You also have legitimate tax deductions for trade association dues, costs of attending meetings, and many other business-related expenses. Your accountant will be able to provide a complete list of deductions applicable to your industry, but you also should consult colleagues and related associations for their suggestions.

#99. **How does an independent contractor claim business deductions?**

Business deductions are part of your income tax forms. If you use a CPA, she will distribute your deductions in the correct slots. If you use your own income tax software, spaces for your deductions will appear on the forms. Just be sure you have a receipt for each deduction you list, in case you are audited.

#100.   As a self-employed person, can I form a 401(k) retirement plan?

Yes—since 2001, self-employed people now can save for retirement in an Individual 401(k). The money invested is tax-free and will grow tax-deferred until the person withdraws it. The account also allows owners to contribute up to 25 percent of their annual pay to themselves. It can be set up with allowances for pre-retirement loans, and in a Roth IRA format, taxing the money as it's deposited and allowing it to grow and be withdrawn tax-free.

#101.   What's the difference between a Roth, Traditional, and SEP Independent Retirement Account (IRA)?

As a self-employed person, you no longer have an employer taking money out of your "paycheck" and investing it in a company retirement plan. Aside from Social Security, independent workers are responsible for funding their own retirement, and one handy savings device is the IRA, or Individual Retirement Account.

In a Roth IRA, contributions are not tax-deductible. The amounts individuals can invest has changed each year; in 2008 it capped at $6,000. Anyone can contribute to an IRA, regardless of their income, and can begin withdrawing funds after age fifty-nine and a half if the funds have remained in the account, untouched, for at least five years.

Contributions to a Traditional IRA usually are tax-deductible, depending on the owner's income and other factors. Dollar limits to contributions are similar to those of Roth IRAs, and withdrawals must start at age seventy and a half.

A SEP IRA is very similar to a profit-sharing plan. Contributions are tax-deductible, and self-employed persons are limited to approximately 18.6 percent of their profit for the year.

#102. **What are the advantages and disadvantages to opening a Roth IRA?**

Advantages of a Roth IRA include tax-free earnings for qualified distributions, and the fact that contributions can be withdrawn at any time, tax- and penalty-free (except for funds converted from a traditional IRA, which are penalized by 10 percent if withdrawn before five years). Earnings also can be withdrawn without being taxed or penalized if the owner has reached age fifty-nine and a half, is buying a first home, or in the event of disability or death.

The primary drawback to a Roth IRA is that during the five years that the money must remain in the account, the money might be needed for a life emergency. That said it is the most popular IRA.

#103. **What are the advantages and disadvantages to opening a Traditional IRA?**

Owners of traditional IRAs enjoy the fact that their earnings grow tax-deferred, and that withdrawals can be made without penalty after age fifty-nine and a half. For younger owners, funds also can be withdrawn for higher education costs, a first-home purchase, death, disability, and some medical and health insurance bills—a broader, more permissive withdrawal policy than with the Roth IRA.

Disadvantages are that deductible contributions and all earnings are taxed as income when withdrawn, contributions must stop at age seventy and a half, and distributions must begin at that time.

#104. **What are the advantages and disadvantages to opening a SEP IRA?**

If you have a small business with several employees, a SEP IRA might be the easiest retirement plan to establish. Contributions are made by the employer only, and don't have to be made every year. Benefits are portable.

However, even part-time employees who've worked three of the preceding five years and earned more than $500 each year must be included in the plan. So, any year in which you, the small business owner, contribute to the plan on your own behalf, you also must make contributions for all qualifying employees.

You can open multiple kinds of IRAs at any combination of lenders that you wish.

#105.   When and how will I start drawing from the IRAs I've opened?

Regulations for each type of IRA specify when the account owner can (or must) begin withdrawing funds. To recap:

- With a Traditional IRA, distributions can begin after age fifty-nine and a half but must begin just after age seventy and a half.
- With a Roth IRA, earnings can be withdrawn under certain conditions if the account owner is at least fifty-nine and a half.
- Distributions from a SEP IRA are penalty-free but taxable after age fifty-nine and a half.

Withdrawals don't happen automatically; you, the account owner, must contact the lenders who hold the accounts and arrange distribution. If you have four IRAs at four different banks, credit unions or investment houses, it is your responsibility to contact each of them at the appropriate time.

#106.   What other options for retirement savings do self-employed people have?

Your savings options are limited only by your imagination. You can choose stocks and bonds, mutual funds, U.S. Savings Bonds, municipal bonds, certificates of deposit, savings accounts, annuities, real estate, an art collection, and you can even choose to hide your money in your mattress. The best choice for you depends on your age, income, interests, and the economy. Every self-employed person should talk with a financial advisor to study your finances and select the savings vehicles that make the most sense for you.

#107. I keep hearing the phrase, "pay yourself first." What does that mean?

In part, it means that a self-employed person should pay himself a fair wage for working so hard; one would hope that wage soon would become competitive for your industry. It also means you should pay yourself sufficiently to make the maximum contributions to your IRA, or to set aside a healthy amount each pay period for other retirement accounts, as well as sufficient funds for personal or business emergencies. It means that addressing your own needs should be a top priority!

#108. Where should a self-employed person invest her retirement funds—in real estate, mutual funds, CDs, or elsewhere?

Oh, wouldn't we love to know that answer! We would sell it at an exorbitant price.

Of course, this is a question everyone needs to resolve, whether they're self-employed or still working for someone else. But the answer may be a bit more elusive for self-employed people because we don't have a company comptroller, or even coworkers, to lean on for advice. We need to figure out these important issues on our own, or hire someone to help us.

The best answer we can give you is to diversify. Try to keep enough cash in a checking account to pay your expenses for a minimum of three months and sufficient money in "cash-able" vehicles, such as short-term CDs and savings accounts, where you can convert it to spendable dollars immediately in an emergency, to cover at least another three months. Withdrawing money from a CD before it matures will cost you in penalties, but if you only buy three-month CDs, and keep much of your emergency cash in a savings account, you won't lose much if you have to cash in one of your CDs. Of course, shop around for the highest interest rates, and be realistic about the amount of cash you'll need for your business—especially during the first year or two.

Beyond those liquid accounts, a financial advisor will tell you to choose the highest interest-earning vehicle that's practical for people your age. If you plan to retire in the next five to ten years, choose low-risk savings; if retirement is decades away, you might want to be more aggressive.

#109.   What retirement options should a small business offer its employees?

Employees of all businesses, including those run by sole proprietors, are required to contribute to either a Social Security retirement fund or a government-sponsored retirement system such as the Public Employees Retirement System (PERS). Beyond those required savings and IRA or 401(k) accounts, employers can offer profit sharing plans and defined-benefit (DB) plans, which can be complex but can offer higher deductible amounts to employers than some other plans. Choosing a retirement plan is an important move for employers, because benefits packages are key in attracting talented employees. Business owners should talk with others in the same industry and similar circumstances to learn how various plans have worked out for them, and consult a financial advisor to help analyze the options.

#110. This retirement business is confusing. Where can a small business owner find (cheap, free) help with financial planning for herself and her business?

All of these agencies and organizations offer help for you:

- The Internal Revenue Service (IRS), *www.irs.gov.*
- The Small Business Administration (SBA), *www.sba.gov.*
- SCORE, *www.score.org.*
- Your local Chamber of Commerce or Growth Association.

#111. How much Social Security income will be available to me by the time I retire?

According to the Social Security Administration's estimates, some 40 million Americans are age 65 or older at this writing. They, and those retirees who follow, will probably exhaust the Social Security Trust Fund by 2040, when it's projected that the number of Americans 65 and older will have doubled, unless the program undergoes significant changes.

Marketing and Selling Your Products and Services

WHEN MOST PEOPLE hear the word, "marketing," they immediately think it refers to magazine and newspaper ads. Yet the differences between advertising, marketing, and public relations, while subtle, are important for a self-employed person to understand.

Part 4 will discuss the finer points of marketing and selling, and where "branding" fits into the picture. A mom starting a tiny bread-making or catering business in her kitchen can be inspired by the soaring popularity of Martha Stewart, the quintessential entrepreneur who became one of America's best-known brands. Martha built her empire from her own kitchen and not only became a billionaire, but forever changed the way we view homemaking in this country.

Martha wasn't the only famous entrepreneur who started small. Ben Cohen and Jerry Greenfield, cofounders of the Ben & Jerry's ice cream empire, took a five-dollar class in ice cream making and opened their first ice cream parlor in a converted gasoline station in Burlington, Vermont. Michael Dell, CEO of the computer company that carries his name, started his company in his living room. And sausage king Bob Evans started by raising his own hogs and making sausage for customers at his diner in Gallipolis, Ohio. All of these success stories grew their businesses with solid business practices, but that wasn't enough to make them household names; that was accomplished with smart marketing.

In this section, we address the specifics of various marketing approaches such as the differences between marketing and PR. E-mail newsletters, traditional networking, the near-volcanic popularity of social networking, and the essentials of a successful website, as well as classic sales and customer service issues, all are addressed here as well.

#112. What's the difference between advertising, marketing, and public relations?

You can see the distinctions between these three terms even in the straight definitions:

- **Advertising** is a paid form of communicating a message through various media—newspapers, magazines, TV, radio, billboards, signs, websites. Advertising is designed to influence purchasing behavior or thought patterns.
- **Marketing** is the activity, institutions, and processes for creating, communicating, delivering, and exchanging offerings that have value for customers, clients, partners, and society. Marketing touches people and puts your business or product in their minds for their future needs.
- **Public relations**, or PR, is a promotion intended to create goodwill for a person or institution. It's also defined as the practice of managing the flow of information between an organization and its publics.

#113. What is a marketing plan, and why does a self-employed person need one?

A marketing plan is your blueprint for making the public aware of your business, products, and services. Many characterize marketing as storytelling—that is, telling your prospective and current customers about your services, and why they are the finest available. A major factor in marketing is researching your customers—what do they want? What can they afford? What do they think about their current choices? Your understanding and applications of such questions will go far in helping your business to succeed.

#114. What are the elements of an effective marketing plan?

A good marketing plan will include the following basics:

1. The purpose and mission of your business.
2. An analysis of your current marketing efforts and circumstances affecting them.
3. Your new marketing strategy, including specific objectives you want to achieve.
4. Specific programs—i.e., how you will go about achieving your objectives; your "action steps."
5. Budgets, timelines, and how you will implement your marketing plan.
6. Additional factors to consider, such as your competition's strengths and weaknesses, and the political and economic environment.

#115. How do I write a press release, and where do I send it?

As writing goes, a press release is relatively easy—it's a statement to the media that conforms to a standard format. Follow these steps:

1. Write the press release on business letterhead, double-spaced, making sure the company's name, website, location, and phone number all are easy to spot near the top.

2. Type the words, PRESS RELEASE, in all-caps and center them at the top of the first page. Next, type the names and phone numbers of contact people, and type IMMEDIATE RELEASE, again in all-caps, along the left margin.

3. Type the title, centered and in boldface. This will be the most creative part of your writing because you need to capture the journalist's attention in one glance. If you are sending press releases by e-mail, then the title should be in the subject line. Make it a title the reporter will want to read about—short and brilliant—and won't delete. (Tip: If you're not "good at titles," try leafing through quality magazines for inspiration, seeing which ad copy gets your attention. You can't duplicate their words, but you can let them inspire your own clever title.)

4. The body of the press release begins with the date and city where the release was written, and flows with the information you want to convey—who, what, where, when, and why. In the first paragraph, state what the release is about, including the most important details.

5. The second paragraph presents, in more detail, why this matters, where the event or product can be found, and when. Insert a quote in this paragraph from the key person regarding the event or product, giving the release a bit of personality.

6. Your third paragraph sums up the information, adding more info about the company and with contact info again listed. Keep the release to a maximum of two pages. At the end, center three "number" or "pound" symbols (###) to indicate that readers have reached the end of the release. And if you have a hard time visualizing the actual release, a simple Google search will give you plenty of examples.

#116. Do I need a website for my business? Why?

A website will make it easy for people to find you, your company, and your products and services. It is a simple and inexpensive way to convey information about you—think of it as your business card.

With a website, you can instantly reach the 1.5 billion people who live on this planet as long as they have access to a computer and you and your products will be as easy for them to find as a huge brands like Pepsi-Cola, Sony, Clorox, or Chevrolet.

#117. What is a domain name, and where do I get one? Can I use it for e-mail, too?

A domain name is the name of your website. It will begin with a World Wide Web prefix (www) and will end with a "dot-com" type of suffix. An example is *www.sheraton.com*. All web addresses follow the same basic format, though today you also could choose a dot-net, dot-biz, dot-tv, or any number of other suffixes.

You can choose and reserve your domain name at any of thousands of hosting companies. Two of the most well known are *www.register.com* and *www.godaddy.com*. When you visit their websites, you will see easy instructions for receiving e-mail through your website; if you have difficulties, their customer service staff can walk you through the set-up.

#118. What is the best marketing tool for a home-based business?

If you could choose only one marketing vehicle, it should be your website. Once you have one, use it to draw as much attention as possible to your business:

- Choose a URL (Uniform Resource Locator—your domain name, or web address) that's intuitive and easy for clients to find and remember, such as *www.marymihaly.com*.
- Include your website on your business cards, e-mail signature, letterhead, and other literature.
- Whenever you speak at conferences, trade shows, or community meetings, always mention your web address.

Later in this section, you'll learn about a host of other low-cost ways to create awareness of your products and services.

#119. How do I build an affordable website? What will it cost me?

If you have an Internet connection, you can build your own website free of charge. Both Microsoft (for PCs) and Apple (for Macs) offer free website-building services. Their instructions are easy to understand, and their customer service staff will get you over any rough spots. You can easily post photos and other images to your site as you build it. Go to *www.microsoft.com* or *www.apple.com* for information.

#120. Are e-newsletters good marketing tools? What are the benefits?

An e-newsletter is a great way to stay in touch with current relationships and share your personality and news with prospective clients. It boosts your reputation and visibility, it's low-cost, and it enables readers to interact with you on the spot.

#121. How do I set up my e-newsletter?

One of the easiest ways to send an e-newsletter is to send a no-frills e-mail. All e-mail programs allow you to create lists, typically of less than 100 e-mail addresses. You can send your brief newsletters by e-mail in batches of 100. The biggest drawback to this method is that you must either retype or cut-and-paste your entire newsletter for each batch.

A much easier option is to send your e-newsletter through an online e-message service such as Constant Contact (*www.constant contact.com*). For a monthly fee, such services will update your list as part of the fee (so that you're not altering the lists yourself every month, adding new addresses and manually deleting those that are obsolete). Many also give you the choice between an all-text newsletter and one that's designed with your logo and other elements you select.

#122.   **What would I write in an e-newsletter?**

Your e-newsletter's content depends on the purpose and audience, but what it should not be is one big advertisement for your business. Try that, and readers will unsubscribe in droves.

Give them content that will make them want to read the next issue. Examples include a brief interview with an expert in the field, industry news and the latest research, your own opinion piece on a subject that's important or provocative in your industry right now, product news that will help readers in their jobs, and/or a collection of tips.

Keep it brief, and always add a bonus giveaway—an extra piece of advice, a special discount on your services, or perhaps even a recipe or joke.

Never reprint something written by another person unless you have their permission; online publishing is publishing nevertheless, and stealing someone's words is illegal. And if writing does not come easily to you, consider hiring a freelance writer for your e-newsletter, brochures, and other editorial needs. A good place to find experienced writers in all fields is the job service of the American Society of Journalists and Authors (ASJA), the country's top trade association of independent nonfiction writers (*www.asja.org*).

#123.   **How do I build a mailing list for my e-newsletter and other online promotions?**

It's not difficult to build a mailing list. Whenever you attend a meeting or social gathering, collect business cards from people you meet and ask them if they'd like to start receiving your free online newsletter. If you include links to other websites in your newsletter where appropriate, those business owners will return the favor; your website should include a place where visitors can subscribe to your e-newsletter and boost your numbers in that way. Another great tool is the social networking boom, which we'll discuss later in this section.

#124. Are blogs valuable for a business?

A blog can be a terrific way to personalize your business in the public eye, and to enable customers to respond and connect with you immediately—but only if you have the time and energy to maintain it and keep it fresh.

Reading and writing blogs can help you track business trends and market your company. But blogs can also invite harsh, even brutal criticism. If you don't want to hear from people who have negative things to say about your products or services, a blog isn't the right marketing tool for you.

Like e-newsletters, blogs shouldn't be advertisements for your business. Successful business blogs are open discussions about industry trends, public issues that affect you and your colleagues, and other business-related topics. They can, however, be operated from your website and can be a handy device for getting potential customers to visit your site. Ask your webmaster how to set up a website-based blog. If you are interested in starting a freestanding blog, you will need a blog host, or blog platform. Some hosts are free, others charge small fees for hosting your blog. You can find three of the more popular blog hosts at *www.blogger.com, www.wordpress.com,* and *www.yahoo.com.*

#125. What's the difference between an e-newsletter and a blog?

An e-newsletter is like a print newsletter, containing information and, sometimes, advertisements. It also can feature opinion pieces.

E-newsletters are sent periodically, but not necessarily according to a strict timeline; they could be produced weekly or monthly, or occasionally if the owner doesn't want to adhere to a schedule. However, if your e-newsletter is going to be an effective marketing tool, clients and prospective clients may expect to see it with some regularity, or they might forget about it—and, consequently, about your business.

A blog can be either informational or opinion, but it is an interactive vehicle, and it is not mailed like the newsletter. The blogger simply writes that day's entry and posts it on his blogsite or website, and readers are invited to respond with their own postings. Like e-newsletters, blogs don't need to follow a strict timeline, but they are expected to contain fresh content. Successful blogs—those with the biggest followings—are updated by the blogger at least once a week.

#126. How can I use e-mail to market myself?

One easy tip: create a tagline for your e-mail signature that mentions your company name and contact info. A well-chosen tagline can serve as a mini-advertisement for your business, every time someone opens an e-mail from you. An example:

Mary Mihaly
Literary Treasures
Cleveland, Ohio
(999) 555-XXXX
www.marymihaly.com

It's acceptable to add one more line if you've just launched a new product or service, but don't make your signature any longer. Obnoxious e-mail signatures annoy people—not a good way to draw customers!

#127. I don't want to send spam—are there guidelines for sending bulk e-mail, such as newsletters?

The classic definition of spam is unsolicited e-mail sent indiscriminately to multiple mailing lists, individuals, or newsgroups. In other words, it's junk e-mail. According to the CAN-SPAM Act of 2005, it's illegal to send spam not only to computers, but also as text and e-mail on "wireless phones and other mobile devices."

The only way to avoid spamming is to get permission from recipients. Your initial e-mail contact should contain links for the person to opt-in if they want to continue receiving your mailings (subscribe), and to opt-out if they don't want to receive any more (unsubscribe). Respect their wishes and you will avoid being blacklisted by the major ISPs (Internet service providers), which would prevent your messages from being delivered.

#128. How can I be sure my e-mails won't be deleted before someone reads them?

The key to getting your e-mails read is in the subject line. Think of that line as a magazine cover: When you stand at a crowded newsstand and look at perhaps a hundred glossy covers in front of you, what makes you reach for one out of that crowd? That's how you should view your subject lines. They determine whether someone will read your messages or throw them away. Make them work with a few irresistible words that make people want to read more.

#129. When is it appropriate to use abbreviations in business-related e-mail?

Your business's messages should reflect your corporate image and client preferences. If your clients work on Wall Street and address each other formally, then it would be best to forego casual language, including abbreviations. But if you cater to teenagers who collect Madonna and Beatles memorabilia, your customers are entirely comfortable with business communications that use "can't," "don't," and "wouldn't." Go ahead and write as if you were talking to them.

#130.   **What should I know about protocol and professionalism in business-related e-mail?**

E-mail has definitely shoved paper aside and taken over as the primary form of business correspondence. But it's still business correspondence, and e-mail should follow your company's image and client preferences in every message. A few basics to keep in mind:

- Your greeting is your handshake; don't omit it. You can't go wrong starting a business e-mail with "Dear Mr. Russell," or "Dear Ms. Kendricks." Even after you get to know the person, "Dear" is a suitable opening and almost never too formal; "Dear Jack" works well as a friendly business greeting.
- Never send a business e-mail without first checking for spelling and grammar. It may not seem as formal as letterhead, but business e-mail still represents you and your business.
- Don't write a book. E-mail has given us weary eyes, and it's easy for the recipient to delete. Be concise and keep it short.
- Include a courteous sign-off. "Sincerely yours," "Best wishes," and other traditional closings are always appropriate.
- Perhaps this goes without saying, but emoticons never should appear in business correspondence, including e-mail.

#131. **What are the legal ramifications of what I write in an e-mail?**

As mentioned earlier, online writing is considered publishing. Legal issues such as plagiarism, slander, libel, and threats of violence all pertain to online writing, including e-mail, as they do to print publishing. Avoid putting anything in writing that you would be reluctant to say in person or publish in a newspaper.

#132. **What is networking, and why is it important to someone working alone in a home office?**

Are clients beating down your door? If not, then you need to feather your business nest and make some connections.

Networking isn't about small talk at a cocktail party; it's about beginning new business relationships that will be mutually beneficial. Especially if you work from home, it's essential to join trade associations and attend seminars, conferences, and mixers where you will meet people who can help your business succeed, and from whom you can learn more about your industry and various aspects of running a business.

#133. **How can I tweak my website to make it a great place where people return, again and again?**

Like your subject lines, websites are another "magazine cover" opportunity to snag readers and keep them. In the first few seconds, viewers will know what they're getting and decide whether they are comfortable with you.

Use the best graphics and images you can afford. If you use photos, make sure they are clear. Focus on drawing attention to the purpose of your site—your purpose and your message—with little distracting "scenery." Animated features that take a long time to load are a turn-off, so skip those—and don't allow your site to become dated or stale. Keep refining and refreshing it.

Spend some time looking at websites of your colleagues and competitors. That exercise will give you an idea of the kinds of elements you want to include, and those you would reject.

#134.   How do I get people to visit my website in the first place?

Experts recommend that you become a "thought leader"—that is, put your name out there electronically, partly by blogging and inserting as many links as possible to websites and other blogs relating to your subject. Owners of those blogs will return the favor, and your blog and site will see a boost in traffic.

You also need to pay attention to search engine optimization—commonly known as SEO—where you try to get your website or blog as high on search engines as possible. If people can find what they're looking for on the first or second page at *www.google.com*, they're not going to continue scrolling for another ten or twenty pages. Obviously, there is great advantage in being listed on the first page.

Your credibility will be enhanced if your website includes testimonials from repeat clients or well-known authorities in your field. Collect testimonials on an ongoing basis and add them to your website and literature. Like blurbs from famous authors on a book cover, testimonials on your website can draw viewers and keep them coming back. As you choose prospective testimonial writers, aim high; if you're selling vitamins, a testimonial from Dr. Andrew Weil will mean more than those from the kindly retired pharmacist who lives on your street. Offer to send literature and samples—don't expect blind endorsements.

Of course, as mentioned earlier, your website's URL, or address, should appear on your business cards and all literature produced by your business. Choose a URL that's easy to remember, either your business name or personal name, and spread the word through all of the networking vehicles discussed in this section, from colleagues to newsletters of trade associations.

#135. How else can I use the Internet to promote my new business?

One of your most dynamic and valuable tools for promotion is the social networking phenomenon. It is a virtual explosion; Facebook alone had as many members in 2009 as the combined populations of Brazil and Japan. It is almost mandatory for anyone with a product or service to maintain a presence on at least two of the many social networking sites available. The biggest drawback is the temptation to spend hours socializing on Facebook, "tweeting" on Twitter, and meeting compadres on LinkedIn, instead of working!

#136. What is LinkedIn, and how do I join?

LinkedIn *(www.linkedin.com)* is by far the most business-oriented of the three top social networking sites. It's used for making professional connections, and to promote your business pursuits. For instance, if I need to interview a female CEO of a manufacturing firm in Nicaragua, I might post my request on LinkedIn. I have access not only to my own connections on the site, but to their connections and *their* connections as well. It is a web of professionals, all carrying on a virtual work relationship.

   As with the other social networking sites, a photo and complete profile will help people to find you and fulfill your requests. You might be asked to forward a connection to one of your contacts; unless you have a good reason for not helping, go ahead and do it—that's why people enrolled. The more you participate, the more likely others will be to help you make connections.

#137. **What is Facebook, and how do I join?**

Once considered a virtual meeting place for teenagers, Facebook *(www.facebook.com)* now is the largest social network, with a decidedly playful atmosphere. Retirees, business owners, job seekers, and anyone else who wants to connect for any reason use Facebook. If LinkedIn is a professional open house, Facebook is the after-work party—but one where you can make and maintain business connections, called "friends." You can "friend" someone with a simple invitation, and privacy settings allow you to keep parts of your profile confidential.

Facebook messages can be forwarded to e-mail accounts, which can annoy people. To answer you, the recipient must log in to Facebook—a double annoyance. Like LinkedIn, Facebook enables many layers of connections, so it can be valuable in networking. You can even treat it as a sort of blog site and build an audience.

#138. **What is Twitter, and how do I join?**

If you think Facebook is too time-consuming, you'd better not go to Twitter *(www.twitter.com)*, because this site can be addicting! The idea is to build a large audience of "followers," which you accomplish by following others, and by "tweeting" often yourself. Each message, or "tweet," must be 140 characters or less, so expect to read a lot of short complaints about cold coffee or babies crying. But you also can use Twitter to bring people along as you plan and develop a project (moment-to-moment, if you like), learn about your industry, and follow individuals whose work interests you, from authors to politicians, corporate figures, and celebrity chefs.

You get from Twitter what you put into it. If you participate and give friendly responses to questions from followers, you will build your own following.

#139. **I'm a shy person. What are some easy, in-person ways to network?**

Shyness can be an obstacle in marketing—even more so if you work at home. Still, networking is essential if you want to keep up with trends in your industry, meet people who can help you be more informed, and stimulate your own ideas. A few ideas:

- Find local business-networking events and meander. Your local chamber of commerce is sure to sponsor a variety of expos, trade shows, and meet-and-greets. Some will be listed in your newspaper. Introduce yourself to vendors and other small-business owners, and listen to what they have to say about the community, the industry, and business opportunities. Be sure to carry a good stash of business cards.

- Be alert for those who can become "working partners." If sales intimidates you, align yourself with a salesperson experienced in your product or service area. There are dozens of ways in which partners from photographers and writers, nurse practitioners and PR people, restaurateurs and plumbers can help you take your business forward, including eventual access to their contacts.

- Volunteer in the community. Most successful businesspeople know that "giving back" not only is good for one's karma, it's also good for your career. Such efforts get you away from your home office and out among people; you can channel your volunteering to follow your own interests. If you love the theatre, volunteer to be an usher at a historic playhouse. People who enjoy caretaking can volunteer with a hospital or the American Red Cross. If you're good with a hammer, Habitat for Humanity always needs volunteers.

- Get active in business groups, or charitable organizations such as the Rotary Club. You'll meet prospective clients, influential business leaders, and interesting colleagues.

#140.   I'm not a "joiner." Why do I need to join trade associations?

You need to join trade associations because no one can thrive in a vacuum. Mentors, clients, idea-sparkers, providers of services you might need, discount suppliers, talented job seekers, all belong to trade associations—maybe to the one you're considering joining. The groups sponsor conferences and trade shows where they present panels of experts, showcase the latest technology, and bring together people who can help each other succeed.

Trade associations also offer opportunities in advocacy, leadership training, continuing education, and mentoring. In every industry and profession, the most successful people belong to trade associations—local, regional, and national.

#141.   I'd like to talk to those with self-employed success stories in my field. Any tips for gaining access to them?

First, do as we've been advising. Leave the office, join associations, collect business cards, engage with the pros. Be proactive in meeting your colleagues, and listen to their experiences and suggestions with enthusiasm.

Join the local chamber of commerce. Attend their mixers and sponsored programs; they will deal with a range of issues that touch your business. When you're ready to call a high-ranking official or very busy person, phone shortly after 5 P.M. when the person's assistant may have just left and he or she may be answering their own phone. They may feel more relaxed at that time of day and more open to conversation and setting up a meeting.

Don't ask for much of their time. Lunch or dinner might be too big a commitment for your first meeting. Propose meeting over coffee, or offer to drop by their office. Have two or three unintrusive questions in mind that will give them an opportunity to advise you in some way.

#142. **How should I view my competitors? I'm not an aggressive person, but I don't want to feel intimidated by the competition, either.**

Competition is a healthy thing; it's about succeeding, not about "beating" another business. If there isn't room in the marketplace for both of you to thrive, you may need to rethink your business plan.

Instead, ask who in your marketplace is not being served, and how can you fill their needs? If you want to start a home-based picture framing business, and you live in a very small town, then there may not be enough of a customer base for two framing shops to survive. But if you are a house painter, and you live in a suburb of Philadelphia, you probably can assume that there's plenty of business for everyone.

Keep in mind, too, that your "community" or marketplace doesn't necessarily mean the town in which you live. A freelance PR specialist in Sacramento can effectively represent clients in New Orleans, Barbados, and Denver, because much of her work is done online.

#143. **How do I distinguish my business from others that provide essentially the same products or services?**

Back when the big box stores were just starting to take over their retail categories, and independent booksellers were wringing their hands over the future of their businesses—and justifiably so, given the huge success of Borders and Barnes & Noble—a wise independent shop owner told me, "There's always a contrarian market. You just have to find it."

She was right. One women's clothing store in Cleveland has stayed in business because the owner found her niche: she's the only high-end clothier who sells quality bathing suits year-round. Women taking a tropical vacation in winter have nowhere to shop but her store. Remember, if the field is crowded, or the bigger companies seem to be closing in, find a niche.

Another way to distinguish your business is to be a "social entrepreneur"—a small business owner who incorporates social values as part of his normal business practices in a big way. Examples include produce brokers who connect local farmers with nearby restaurants, "upcyclers" who keep reusable items out of landfills by finding new homes for them, and Internet sellers of handcrafted items made by women in impoverished rural areas. Such companies can make healthy profits while helping others earn a living at the same time.

#144. As a self-employed person, do I need a logo for my business?

If you are a sole proprietor working from home, you may not need a logo—but it doesn't hurt to have a special symbol that will impress people and help them to remember you.

If you own a retail business or have a similar "public face," your business should have a logo. It's another way to stand out from the crowd—who doesn't recognize that green circle as Starbucks, or you-know-who's golden arches? Anyone who bakes can open a bakery, but if you want customers to think of you first when they need an elegant, prize-winning cake for a special occasion, a logo will help your business come to mind.

#145. How do I design or choose a memorable business card?

If you have a logo, it should be featured in your business card's design. Your card should have a clean look; don't clutter it by filling the space with words. Use the reverse side of the card if you need to list products or services. Also, your card's design should complement the design of your letterhead stationery.

If you don't know a graphic designer who will design your card for an affordable fee, visit your local print shop or chain copy shop. They have notebooks of sample designs; you should be able to find one that's compatible with your business and personality.

#146. When are other kinds of promotional items—bookmarks, scratch pads, pens—useful?

People love getting freebies, but unless you are running for political office or promoting a book you've authored, these products probably won't generate customers. Unless I already love a winery's wine, drinking from their souvenir glass wouldn't convince me to buy a bottle of it. I've always thought that such items were more useful in evoking fun memories than drumming up return business. That said, if I were in Napa Valley and couldn't recall the name of a wine I once enjoyed there, having the souvenir glass at home would remind me of the name and I might stop at that winery to buy a bottle.

#147. Are there any unusual ways of networking or marketing myself that my competitors don't know about?

Your competitors probably aren't "hypercommuting," which is done with a "smart phone." Hypercommuting enables you to download or access any document in your desktop. You could be at your son's soccer game and need to send a document somewhere; instead of rushing to the office or hauling your laptop around, you can use your cell phone to send the file. The phones are relatively pricey—several hundred dollars, plus hefty monthly service fees—but if you truly are torn between spending time with your family and dealing with clients in other time zones, hypercommuting could be the answer.

#148.   **What is "viral marketing"? It sounds contagious.**

Exactly! Viral marketing is an idea that people can't resist passing on. In days of yore, television was the medium for viral marketing because it exposed us to ads that tugged at our hearts or made us laugh. Do you remember the lyrics, "I'd like to teach the world to sing in perfect harmony…?" Was there ever a more appealing sentiment or a catchier tune used in an ad? For a few months, we all wanted to "buy the world a Coke and keep it company." And were Wendy's burgers really superior to those sold by the fast-food competition, or did we buy them because we thought Dave Thomas was a cute old guy?

At this writing, YouTube probably is the medium for launching a company's viral marketing, and every self-employed person has access to it.

#149.   **How will I know the ROI (return on investment) for my networking efforts?**

You can measure your networking success in meaningful ways. If you work from a home office, indicators of your networking success probably will be readily apparent. A surge in business following a trade show or an advertisement should tell you whether your investment was worth repeating.

Other successes are more difficult to track. That's why Priceline asks you to fill out an online survey every time you use their services, and why many restaurants place response cards on their tables. Sometimes, the best way to learn how customers found you, how they feel about their experience with you, whether they would do business with you again and, importantly, whether they would recommend your business to a friend, is simply to ask them. Consider occasionally including a very brief survey in your e-newsletter.

#150. How can I improve the outcomes of my networking?

Do this by being selective about your networking efforts. You may not need to be on all the social networking sites; talk to colleagues about what works best for them, and consider investing more energy into just one of the sites.

As you ease up on networking vehicles that don't bring results, put more energy into those that do. Instead of an all-text e-newsletter, for instance, upgrade to one with a design. If the results from attending one conference or trade show don't seem to justify the time and expense, research similar events and try one; you may have selected an expo in a location that doesn't make sense for your business, or whose attendees aren't likely clients for some reason.

Networking and marketing are not one-time efforts; they are processes that need to be continually refined.

#151. How often should I update my contact lists and mailing lists? Are there easy ways to do that job?

For print mailings, you should update the list every time a piece of mail is returned to you as undeliverable. Your address or label-making software should utilize an easy process for adding new addresses and eliminating those that no longer work.

For online mailing lists, an e-mail delivery service such as Constant Contact (*www.constantcontact.com*) automatically updates your lists with every mailing; it deletes addresses when mail is returned and adds new ones whenever you send them.

#152. How do I set fees for my services?

This question is constantly discussed in every trade association whose members provide services. The simple-yet-complex answer is to set a range that takes into account your location, the rates set by colleagues, the difficulty of the work, and occasionally the client's budget.

Keep in mind that location matters. A freelance wedding photographer in New York City whose clients include TV celebrities can charge much higher fees than a wedding photographer in Des Moines. Many clients are more comfortable paying a set rate for certain types of jobs; others prefer to pay by the hour. It makes sense to set slightly lower fees for clients who send you plenty of work and don't insist on too many revisions—but do let them know you are giving them a discount, and don't under-sell yourself. Ask colleagues in your area how much they charge, and consider a friends-and-family fee that's substantially lower than for other clients, in case they need your help on occasion. Such a discount sends a message that you cannot work for free and that this is your livelihood, and guards against you feeling resentment over being manipulated into giving free labor.

#153. What does "branding" mean? Why is it important?

When a name or symbol distinguishes a product or service in your mind from its competitors, that name or symbol also is a brand. When you hear the words Oprah or Febreze or Tums, certain images come to mind because they are brands. They all have competition, but they stand out.

That is your marketing goal—to stand out among your peers, so that your prospective clients think of your business as the one that can best fill their needs. When you become a brand, a promise of excellence and fulfillment is implied. Living up to that expectation is the vision that will get you to brand status.

#154. How can I get my clients to refer me to other prospective clients?

There are only two ways to entice clients to refer you to others. One is to exceed their expectations of you. If you deliver excellence on time, or even early, you can be sure of their referral.

The other method is to ask. When they compliment you on a job well done, let them know you're grateful for their confidence in you, you hope to work with them again soon, and you would appreciate their referring their friends or colleagues when they have a need.

#155. Do you have a networking tip that will increase my business?

Be generous-hearted. Don't hoard names of suppliers or clients who need more than you can provide. Share your contacts, information, and wisdom, especially after you've been in business for a while and are asked by someone just starting out. Don't give away the store, but building a reputation as one who happily lends a hand, rather than one who is cutthroat, will serve you well as you build your business.

#156. When are thank-you gifts for clients appropriate?

A simple, verbal thank-you is appropriate whenever someone displays a kindness or does you a small favor. And, as a self-employed person, you will score points with a handwritten thank-you note if a colleague or client buys a meal or goes out of their way to meet with you.

A thank-you gift should be reserved for special occasions. For Christmas or Hanukkah, a small gift for faithful clients, or for individuals who have referred business to you during the year, is a great idea. But don't shower clients with gifts, and don't feel that you have to spend much money. A food gift or basket makes a great impression; buy it from a local company—or, even better, make it yourself.

#157. How can I get publicity for my new business?

We already discussed press releases. Many entrepreneurs believe that even more effective are editorial stories published about you in newspapers and magazines. And here's a tip: every reporter in the world is constantly on the lookout for good story ideas. They're not going to interview you just because you're starting a business. But if you have found a true niche, or are distinguishing your business by training underprivileged students or buying all-organic materials, you might get their attention.

Call them personally, ask briefly if they would like to see some materials about your new business, and then drop it off in person if possible. Win them over with a smile and offer to talk with them at their convenience. Take the same approach with local radio and TV talk show hosts and other personalities. But think of a way—several ways, if possible—to stand out from other local businesses that produce the same services or products. Be the first to do something, or the most award-winning, or the most courageous. Sponsor an event the media can't ignore. Don't be just another t-shirt store.

#158. What is strategic networking?

Strategic networking is a way of fine-tuning your networking efforts. Unlike most people's idea of networking—broadcasting their message to as many people as possible, and handing out business cards to almost everyone they meet—strategic networking involves making contacts with prospective clients and making that first conversation as meaningful as possible. Rather than selling them on your own background and services, the idea is to listen to them instead, asking questions and gathering information. When you leave them, you have a much better idea as to whether they will eventually be your clients.

#159. How do I engage prospective clients?

Even though it may seem counterintuitive as a network strategy, collect all the business cards you can from prospective clients without worrying how many of your own you give away. As you get into a conversation, ask questions about people's biggest concerns regarding their business and current problems they need to solve. If they have business needs of their own that are unresolved, such as hiring reliable help, make a mental note of it.

At some point, let them know where the services you offer might intersect with the solutions they seek. Don't try to get them to commit as clients, but follow up and stay in touch. They may not use your services this year, but if you continue the relationship in a nonintrusive way, you will be on their minds when they do finally decide to go after the kind of help you could provide.

#160. If a prospective client's needs seem urgent or troublesome, how can I secure them as a client without waiting for months?

Show them you know what you're doing by following up with an idea they can use this week. It can be a stand-alone idea that came from you, or one you've read recently in a trade magazine; either way, they'll know you are a problem-solver.

#161. **I've never advertised before—are there basic advertising guidelines for promoting my product or services?**

The experts advise small businesses to use only one message in their ads. Some years ago, the tourism office of Costa Rica used the message, "No Artificial Ingredients" in their ads targeting leisure travelers. They were the first to capitalize on a destination's eco-friendly policies to increase tourism, and the ad campaign was tremendously successful.

It's also important that your ads make it easy to find your business. A website or e-mail address will make your small business more accessible and "human," which is part of the appeal of small businesses.

#162. **How do I hire salespeople when I don't have a background in sales?**

You're hiring salespeople precisely for that reason—because it's not your area of expertise, and you need someone with those skills. Learn as much as you can about their experience, skills, and strengths, and why they believe they can succeed in selling your products or services. Several other points to explore in your interview include:

- Find out why they are in sales in the first place. You're looking for someone who is highly skilled, but who also is likeable and appears trustworthy because your salespeople might be the primary contacts for your customers. Answers to this question will help you know whether you like an applicant.
- What are the person's other passions, outside of sales?
- What do they like and dislike about the sales process?

#163. **How and where can I learn some sales basics?**

You really don't need to educate yourself about becoming a professional salesperson. If sales makes you uncomfortable or doesn't come naturally to you, learn about marketing and promotion instead. Focus your energies on creating excellence and making your customers and clients happy, and the sales will come.

#164. **How do I become more visible in my community? Will that help my business?**

People enjoy supporting one of their own, so becoming an active part of the community can help your business immensely.

Volunteer when you can—and if you make a commitment to a volunteer gig, show up. Build a reputation as being a person of your word. If you're a person of religious beliefs, attend a church or synagogue. Show up at community events—arts and crafts fairs, restaurant openings, sporting events, among others. Give talks at organizational meetings when you can, and try to sit on the board of trustees of at least one nonprofit organization.

#165. **How do I find clubs and other organizations that would invite me to speak at their meetings and events?**

It's a matter of letting them know you're available, and briefing them on your expertise. Compile a contact list using ads and news stories from local papers, recommendations from friends, and even the Yellow Pages. From retirement groups to gardening clubs, most organizations are always on the lookout for speakers with interesting information.

#166. How do I approach clubs and other organizations to offer my services as a speaker?

Send them a letter by snail mail, explaining that you're the owner of a new small business and would love to increase your visibility in the area by talking to their group at an upcoming meeting.

However, it's important that they know you won't spend that time talking about yourself and your business. If you are a financial advisor speaking to a group of retired people, talk to them about financial issues that affect them in their retirement. If you are a graphic designer talking to a group of business owners, give a talk on the elements of an attention-getting logo or sign. Hand out a business card or informational handouts to everyone in the audience; if they are impressed by your expertise, they'll call you when they need someone with your skills.

#167. Are there other ways to give to the community that might also be good for business?

One excellent method is to donate a small portion of proceeds to a local charity. Each November and December, my hair stylist donates 5 percent of all money she takes in for gift cards to a local free clinic. It's a gesture that helps the clinic immensely, but it also boosts her business during those months. She sends a monthly e-newsletter to clients, and her October, November, and December issues mention the donation. Not only is she helping the clinic, but her clients feel as if they're donating as well.

#168. Why should I get on the board of trustees of a nonprofit organization?

First, sitting on boards is good for business. It tells people that, although you are a business owner who wants to earn profits, you also care about animals, the arts, a faith-based effort, or people who aren't in such fortunate circumstances.

You also learn a great deal from serving on boards. When I was a trustee for a local mental health center, I was asked to be a part of the center's union negotiations—a fascinating episode that taught me lessons I've used in many aspects of my business.

Serving on boards is also a way of giving back to the community that has supported you, personally and professionally. Being a leader of a charitable organization helps people, and it's good for the soul.

#169. How do I become a board member?

The most successful board members—that is, those who stay long-term, accomplish much for the organization, and enjoy the experience—are those who followed their own interests in choosing a board. Whether you care deeply about protecting wildlife, promoting medical research, keeping a local river clean, or some other cause, try to get on boards whose missions you already support.

Be active in the organization. Volunteer not only for special events, but year-round. Get to know staff and current board members and, when a vacancy occurs, talk with the officers and let them know you're interested. You probably won't have to wait long; most boards require a turnover every few years. If it is a membership organization, such as a trade association, you may have to be elected to fill a seat.

#170. What's the best way to handle customer complaints?

Most unhappy customers will complain in person, on the spot, rather than write a letter or phone call after they leave. Create a spirit in the office that welcomes all customer feedback, and try to anticipate negative comments before they come in. When you do have an unhappy customer:

- Be positive, professional and polite. Focus on what can be done about the problem, not on defending your business or your staff. Your aim is one more satisfied—if not entirely happy—customer.
- Take full responsibility for whatever went wrong. The customer, as they say, is always right.
- Propose a solution. If that doesn't work, keep compromising and proposing.
- Compensate the customer. If a full cash return isn't practical, offer a discount for the future.

#171. I spend way too much time in servicing small customers. How can I learn about more efficient customer service?

We all know why good customer service is important: because it keeps customers coming back. How to accomplish that can be a problem for cash-strapped small business owners, especially sole proprietors.

Insurance representatives and others who deal in personal service, such as financial consultants, typically encounter the difficulty of balancing good customer service with the need to constantly bring in new business. If you spend too much time chasing down details to keep customers and clients happy, it may be time to invest in some help. It needn't cost that much; college interns can answer the phone for you, earn a small wage, and get practical experience from a pro. They can answer preliminary questions, take your messages, make appointments, and help you around the office. We'll have more to say about hiring assistants in Part 5.

PART 5

Time, Energy, and Personal Considerations

WORKING FOR YOURSELF, especially alone in a home office, can be a lonely and sometimes frightening journey. Motivating yourself to get in there and start working can feel like mountain climbing, especially on a sunny morning when neighbors are outside, sharing a mug of coffee and a little gossip.

It's not always easy to schedule your day when it has no built-in structure and not everyone is good at handling that much flexibility. Spouses sabotage your day, kids barge into the office, you have deadlines but can't force yourself to work through your fatigue—these are universal problems among self-employed people.

This section will offer solutions to those obstacles. You'll also learn how to keep your energy levels high, find your best work times, and hire an intern or assistant—and, even more baffling for some sole proprietors, how to put them to work.

#172.   **I'm a sole proprietor, working out of my home—where can I find others to share ideas with?**

We discussed joining trade associations and networking in Part 4, but sometimes you need to communicate with colleagues on a closer, more personal level.

One option is Monday morning, start-the-week breakfasts. Band together with four or five colleagues and commit to meeting for breakfast every Monday to talk shop. Make it early—7 A.M. is a good start time—so it doesn't eat into your workday; the point is to launch a great work week, not avoid it.

A little socializing at these breakfasts is fine, but stick to work topics as much as possible. This "breakfast bunch" can be your best support group. Use them to sound out new ideas, announce your goals for the week, and brainstorm solutions to problems.

If you are friendly with peers in other cities, you might try a phone version of the Monday morning breakfasts. I know of several such phone groups that "meet" on Friday afternoons to assess their progress for the week, but I see more value in the Monday morning approach.

You can also ask a colleague to be your "goal buddy." This is especially helpful if you are in a profession that is by nature solitary, such as writing. Goal buddies can either set regular times to talk, or keep the structure open-ended, but they should talk at least once a week to check their progress, anticipate possible problems, and talk about ways of resolving them.

#173.   **I just set up my home office. How can I keep my family from coming in here and disturbing me all the time?**

Locks work—unless you also are responsible for a child's care, in which case you may need to recruit a babysitter, at least part-time.

One way to persuade your family to respect your business boundaries is to have a family meeting and tell them how important it is that you are "at work" when you're working. Kids may not understand your new arrangements; they're not accustomed to having you at home but not available to them. But your work time and space have to be respected or you won't get much done.

The ideal arrangement is a door that closes; when the door is shut, you are at work. The experts at SCORE offer a few suggestions for setting home office boundaries:

- No interruptions unless it's urgent.
- No playing with office equipment, or answering your business phone.
- No fighting, screaming, or loud music or TV during working hours.
- Keep pets out of the office.

#174. How can I tactfully handle friends and family who think that because I'm self-employed, I'm always available?

When they call to chat during working hours, you can tell them it's great to hear their voice, but you're on your way to meet a client. Or you're working on something you must finish by the end of the day and will call them back after 6 p.m.? Or, if you honestly feel like taking a break, tell them you can spare five minutes but then you do have to get back to what you were working on.

After you use these "I'm-at-work" responses a few times, they should realize that you do have a job and can't fool around during the day. Or, if they fail to get the message, you may need to tell them directly, "It's difficult for me to gab during working hours, because I really do have to earn a living at this. It's always easier if you call in the evening." And, unless it's a business meeting, don't "do lunch." It's too difficult to get back to work after you've had a couple of hours of midday fun.

#175.   **How can I handle friends and family who expect free or discounted services just because I'm self-employed?**

Why not give them a friends-and-family discount? They're not going to engage your services that often. Offer a 25 percent discount; that keeps it businesslike and you won't feel as if they're taking advantage of you. If it turns out that they do want to use your services on a regular basis, inform them firmly but nicely that you've been giving them a hefty discount, and you'll need to negotiate a higher rate.

#176.   **As a sole proprietor, I feel as if I'm working all the time, and I feel guilty if I take time off. How can I balance my personal and business lives?**

Managing your time, and forcing yourself to take time off, is a dilemma for most self-employed people. A few tips:

- Don't multitask with domestic chores when you're working; it will make you feel fragmented. In fact, many successful home-based professionals hire someone to clean their house. They don't consider it an extravagance; dust and dirt are distracting, and they're more productive when they hire someone to take care of the dirt.
- Take a break when your energy is low. Walk, or in bad weather, walk in place while you watch a talk show for half an hour. Give yourself a chance to rejuvenate.
- Get dressed. Get out of your sleep pants and at least put on jeans and shoes. It will make you feel more as if you're "at work."
- Except in rare instances, keep regular work hours. Don't work into the night, or more than six days a week, unless you have a crushing deadline and have no choice.

#177. **How can I stay focused and enthusiastic about my new business?**

This, too, is where regularly meeting or talking with colleagues serves you well. We all get tired of our jobs, but other people's enthusiasm can be contagious. A goal buddy can keep you engaged with your work, too. And if your Monday breakfast group lapses into prolonged negativity about their jobs, and evolves into little more than a weekly gripe session, consider leaving that group and starting another. You don't want to start the week on a negative note—you need to surround yourself with upbeat, forward-looking professionals who want to excel in their jobs.

#178. **I need to exercise, but can't leave my home office for two hours to go to the gym. How can I exercise at home, and incorporate it into my work day?**

Exercising many times throughout the day, rather than one hour-long workout, can be just as effective in terms of fitness and weight loss. Take ten- or fifteen-minute walks in the neighborhood, or run in place in front of the TV. If there are stairs in your home, walk up and down the stairs for ten minutes. Buy some free weights and and do some curls or other arm exercises for a few minutes at a time. Make it a habit to get out of your seat every time you talk on the phone and walk in place.

If you can spare half an hour, build a small library of exercise and yoga DVDs and use those. When I need a break from the computer, I often pop one of trainer Lesley Sansone's walking videos into the DVD player; usually I reach for one that incorporates free weights and other upper-body exercise into the walking workouts. A treadmill is a sound investment if you have the space and enjoy walking; keep a water bottle and your MP3 player at the treadmill and hop on for ten-minute jaunts whenever you feel stiff or tired.

#179.   **Working from my home office, I don't eat right anymore and often feel sluggish. How can I keep my energy high?**

One of the most important ways to keep energy high all day is to eat breakfast. When you skip breakfast, it's too easy to overindulge at lunch and be sluggish the rest of the day. Make your first meal a "power meal"—protein, fruit, or complex carbohydrates such as oatmeal, which takes longer to absorb in your system than dense carbs like bagels or pastries (and won't cause your glucose levels to spike).

During the day, eat whole grains, proteins, fruits, and vegetables. Stay away from dense carbs, sugar, greasy foods, or too much coffee. If you like to eat energy bars, read the labels carefully and make sure they don't contain too much sugar or sodium. And take a daily multivitamin; it will help keep you energized and focused.

#180.   **I'm easily distracted, and I know the TV in the next room will be a constant temptation. How do I discipline myself to work all day?**

Look at your working style. Does your flexible schedule make you feel lazy? If so, think about keeping to a traditional eight-hour workday. Or, you might do well using what's called a "consolidated work week," in which you consolidate a five-day work week into three or four days, working longer hours and rewarding yourself with full days off.

You also might look at your morning ritual. At what point do you actually feel that the work day has begun? Is it after you read your e-mails? After you take a morning walk and shower? Identify the moment when you feel you are "at work" for the day, and really start your work day then. You might even say out loud, "Okay—I'm on the job now!" No more distractions or procrastinating—you are at work.

#181. **Now that I'm working at home, how can I minimize the feeling of isolation that sometimes creeps in?**

We've discussed the importance of networking and talking often with colleagues. It really is helpful to feel that you are part of a work community. You now no longer socialize around the water cooler, and feeling that loss is a surprise to many self-employed people.

And, just because you have made it clear to family and friends that you can't play during the work day, that doesn't mean you can't contact them during your breaks. A break is just that—a brief time to set aside work and refresh yourself—and there's nothing wrong with calling a friend or family member for a ten-minute call.

Sometimes, too, it helps just to walk outside for a few minutes, take in the fresh air, and say hello to neighbors. No matter how many clients you have, in how many cities or countries, working in a home office tends to shrink your world. You need to see that it's only your imagination.

#182. **How can I motivate myself to network when I don't feel like it?**

Sometimes, when you don't interact with colleagues for a little while, it's more difficult to emerge from your office-cocoon and stoke those fires.

Networking isn't a chore that you make yourself perform from time to time. The best way to prevent ambivalence about this important work activity is to make it part of your work day. Every day, do at least one thing that would be considered networking, whether it's meeting with your Monday breakfast group, registering for a work-related expo, following up on an article you read in your trade association's newsletter, or making an appointment to meet a fellow entrepreneur for the first time.

#183. **I have two employees—how do I motivate them to network? Are there motivational tools I can offer them?**

What you're really asking your employees to do, in wanting them to network on behalf of your business, is to show support for both them and for you.

If they are to help you maintain business relationships, you will have to boost their sense of ownership in their jobs. Regardless of their job titles, acting as the face of the company calls for professionalism. They will have to exhibit that quality, and you probably will need to upgrade your image of them as well.

Incentives help employees feel that they are working in a career, rather than just a job. You needn't spend a fortune; lunch in a white-tablecloth restaurant, or even a preloaded Starbucks gift card, can go a long way in making your staff feel that their work is important. Have one-on-one meetings with them, and share some details regarding the operation. Ask for their suggestions in meeting selected challenges, and show your appreciation when they share their insights.

Making their lives easier in little ways will also help breed professional loyalty. Fix the printer, install the lighting they say they need in their work areas, and make sure female staffers aren't walking to their cars alone after dark.

And, let them see your passion for your own work. It's bound to be contagious.

#184. **How can I get better at remembering people's names?**

Here are four quick tips:

1. Each time you meet someone, repeat his or her name out loud. After you're finished talking, repeat the name to yourself two or three more times.

2. Make eye contact with the person as you repeat the name.
3. Pay attention to the person's facial features and use them as a funny nickname, known only to you. I've been introduced to Clarence Cleft-chin, Eric Eyelashes, and Nancy Neck.
4. Ask for a business card. When you're handed the card, repeat the full name one more time, and any other identifying notes such as title or company.

#185.   **Where can I learn to be a good negotiator?**

A good negotiator is a good planner, thinks clearly and quickly under stress, has high self-confidence, and is a good communicator. Here are three online resources that can help you develop those skills:

- *www.amanet.org,* the website of the American Management Association, sponsors courses across the country.
- *www.ThinkOnYourFeet.com* offers training in business communications, including negotiating, with classes in cities across the U.S.
- *www.NegotiationSkills.com* offers workshops and individual consulting in negotiating.

#186.   **I want to get out there and promote my business. How do I get over my fear of public speaking?**

Realize, first, that the audience is on your side. They want you to succeed.

Your best weapon, then, is to be thoroughly prepared. Make sure your notes are organized, highlighted, and marked in whatever way will help you give a smooth talk. Rehearse at home, in front of a mirror. Arrive early, talk to a few people, and make sure that all of your equipment works. Leave nothing to chance.

Smile, and watch the audience smile back at you. Pick out a few friendly faces in different parts of the room, and talk to their foreheads.

Don't forget to breathe. Take several deep breaths before you speak, and an occasional deep breath during your talk. You'll feel as if those breaths are long pauses, but they'll seem perfectly normal to the audience.

#187. How can I learn to be a better public speaker?

There is no better "school" for public speaking than Toastmasters International *(www.toastmasters.org)*, a nonprofit educational organization with some 235,000 members in more than 105 chapters worldwide. Membership is divided about equally between men and women, with about one-third reporting incomes over $100,000 annually—so even the most successful people feel they can use help with their public speaking. Even more relevant to you, about 20 percent of members are self-employed.

By joining Toastmasters, you not only will learn to be a better speaker, you will become a more persuasive, more confident speaker as well. You will be assigned a mentor and will be asked to give a four- to six-minute talk within a few weeks. Fellow members will give you encouragement and helpful feedback.

#188. I run a family business. How do I keep family relations separate from business issues?

Families who work together don't always stay together. Some studies of family business dynasties have found that, typically, it is the third generation, the grandchildren of the founders, who base many of their family relationships in the courtroom.

In a family business, it's important to keep business matters at work, and to avoid bringing family issues into the business. That's easier said than done. It's helpful to hold family members to the same standards as other employees; if they haven't earned a promotion, they shouldn't receive one.

Still, families are intense little communities, especially when money and power are at play. Don't hesitate to see a family counselor who's experienced in family businesses.

#189. Should I start a business with my spouse? What are the pitfalls of a husband/wife business?

Being together at work and at home could be a blessing or a curse. Small disputes and annoyances tend to magnify when people spend too much time together.

Working together introduces new sources of stress into the relationship. Before, you only had your home life as the setting and reason for disagreements. As business partners, much more is at stake and if business slows, it's easy to blame the other partner.

However, marriage and business can work well together—after all, you already know each other's skills and personalities—if you set certain ground rules. Decide which of you will have the final say in disagreements, and vow to communicate constantly about both business and personal issues. Boundaries and responsibilities should be clearly defined, and you should commit to a "marriage life" outside the office—pairing as business partners shouldn't happen at the expense of your marital relationship. Also, be aware of changes in tax requirements when you hire a spouse.

#190. Is it a good idea to hire other family members, such as adult children?

Children of business owners can be an asset to the business. You know their talents, and you can be sure of their loyalty. However, their expectations may be different from those of other staff; they may feel entitled to higher salaries and top positions. It's extremely difficult to fire a family member, or even a good friend. You can head off trouble, though, with a few simple rules:

- Only hire family members for jobs for which they are qualified, at salaries other employees in those jobs receive.
- Hold a family meeting to go over your philosophy of hiring family and your criteria for them.
- Insist that the family member work for another company—in particular, for another boss—before working for you.
- Arrange the flow of authority so that your child reports to a non-family member. The last thing you want is for your child to come running to Mommy or Daddy when things don't go her way.

#191. **What are some tips, day by day, that will help me prevent burnout and keep me feeling balanced?**

If you're drained of energy and every day seems like a bad day, you may be experiencing burnout. Some tips for avoiding it include:

- Start your day in a relaxing way. Do a little yoga, read some fiction, write in your journal. Don't just jump out of bed and start working.
- Get enough sleep, do thirty minutes of deliberate exercise every day, and eat healthy foods.
- Respect your own boundaries. Don't accept every assignment or say yes to every job.
- Do something creative. Put away the technology and pick up some watercolors or woodworking tools. Force yourself out of your work-and-sleep rut.
- Nurture your relationships. Call an old friend, play with a niece or nephew, tell someone you appreciate him or her. The next time you have dinner with a friend, take flowers.

#192. How can I keep my clients in an economic downturn? I can't afford to charge them less.

That's good, because when times are tough, discounts can be dangerous, especially in service professions. People will expect the discounts to continue; they won't want to pay full price again and you risk moving your business down-market.

Instead of charging clients less, give them something more. If you're a resume-writing service, offer to critique their current resume for free. In other fields, you might offer to give clients a free thirty-minute consultation, or product samples.

#193. I find I can't run my home-based business alone. Can a college intern help me?

Yes, you probably can use a college intern. Most schools (and students) now expect payment for their work; the amount depends on local regulations and the school's internship programs. Expect to pay at least minimum wage, and have a space ready where the intern can work.

There is paperwork involved in enlisting the help of an intern and sometimes meetings with an instructor or the student's advisor—again, the amount of work involved depends on the school. It would be better, first, for you to figure out what you need, including how many hours you need someone there, qualifications you would require of the intern, and details such as transportation for the student if you don't live near the school.

#194. What kind of work could an intern do for me?

Think first of simple office tasks that distract you or take your time: photocopying, filing, running errands, and answering the phones. Then there are the more sophisticated office jobs, which you may or may not want to trust to an intern, such as answering e-mails, proofreading correspondence, writing your e-newsletter, and preparing handouts and special mailings.

#195.   I want to start a catering business in my home. Where can I learn about health ordinances, inspections, and other regulations that would affect me?

Check with your city's health department, located in city hall or the county administration building. Their staff will provide lists of regulations for your type of business. You must also consult the town's zoning department to make sure you will be allowed to operate the business from your home, and whether you need a special permit.

#196.   Should I set regular business hours for my new company?

If your clients, customers, and suppliers work regular business hours, then you need to be available during those times as well. Beyond that consideration, you can be open for business whenever you like. As you start out, pay attention to patterns in your energy, your moods, and your ability to focus throughout the day. You may want to shift the way you structure the day, based on what you discover.

#197.   I'm a single parent with a child at home. Can I realistically start a home-based business now, or should I wait until my kid is in school?

Thousands of single parents, kids in tow, successfully run home-based businesses. Think about keeping it to part-time in the beginning, until you know your energy flow throughout the day, the kids' attitudes about your working at home (and bestowing your attention elsewhere, not on them), cash flow, building a client base, and other factors that aren't easy to gauge until you're in business.

Also, consider getting help. Even if you only can afford a nanny or babysitter part-time, you can save that time for scheduling errands and client meetings. If grandparents or other family members are available for babysitting duty, bring them in. With just one child left at home, your juggling soon will get a bit easier and you can transition into full-time.

Managing Ongoing Success

THE CHALLENGES OF being self-employed don't stop after you've survived start-up. They can be managed, however, with relative ease.

Evaluating your business success—and yourself as an effective boss if you have employees—should be a top priority, along with constant upgrading of your own skills and knowledge. Entrepreneurs need to develop the ability to anticipate fast changes in technology and regulations, and to adjust to global shifts without stumbling.

Part 6 discusses these aspects of being self-employed in this fast-paced society, and how business owners should invest profits back into the business so they are always prepared for changes. We will also air the all-important rule of self-employment: Never become complacent.

#198. Aside from watching my checking account grow, how should I evaluate the success of my business?

We mentioned earlier how some businesses, such as restaurants and hotels, leave comment cards to try to assess how customers feel toward them. For self-evaluation, there's a more straightforward approach: pull out your business and marketing plans, and check your business's progress against your goals and objectives—after all, that's why you wrote them.

Has the business been meeting most of its deadlines, for example? If the answer is "yes," ask yourself whether the reason is because you're good at time management, or because you're working 24/7 and finishing jobs early. If you're working too many hours, adjust your pace and take time to relax; if you're under- or overestimating the time it takes to do a job, adjust your deadlines or workload. Look at the goals for your employees, too, and check their progress. In fact, their files should contain employee evaluations, updated once a year.

#199. How can I self-evaluate my performance as the owner and leader of my business?

Once a year, take a step back and ask yourself: Am I still the person to take this company forward? Would I be willing to fire myself? What about my ability to handle risk—have I gotten better at it over the past year?

It's difficult to quantify your own progress, so aside from matters mentioned earlier, such as meeting deadlines and reaching financial goals, you need to force yourself to be objective. One approach is to write down the essentials of your company a year from now—annual revenues, number of employees, clients, whichever measures you care about. Make a detailed plan to get from Point A, where you and the business are today, to Point B—the sketch of your business a year from now.

Then look at your revenues, employees, and clients today and ask yourself: What are the behaviors and attitudes that kept you from following that path in the past? Those are the behaviors you need to improve.

#200.   How do I know if self-employment is still the best choice for my life?

Robert Half International, the world's largest specialized staffing firm, devised a quiz published on the jobs website, *www .careerbuilder.com,* that measures your interest in your job. It asks such questions as, "You're on a weeklong vacation. There's an Internet café at your hotel. How often do you check in with the office?" The questions measure your passion for your job, the extent to which you're a workaholic, whether you've switched jobs too often, and other indicators.

The fact is, even self-employed people make career mistakes—or, if they're lucky, their self-employment puts them in the best possible job situation. If you find yourself caring less and less whether the work gets done, or avoiding your office to become a couch spud, then you may need to talk to a counselor or job coach about what's missing from your work life, and whether you should move on.

#201.   When should I hire employees for my home-based business?

It may be time to hire some help, either part-time or full-time when you're working those long hours with no time for family or friends, and you feel overwhelmed with stress. If you're close to making that decision, the first person you should call is your accountant, to educate you about the various taxes you need to withhold from the new employee's paycheck. You also need to decide whether you will offer employee benefits such as health insurance, paid vacation, and sick leave.

Don't hire a clone of yourself—you need someone to complement your skills, not duplicate them. If the person you want to hire is undecided, offer a small signing bonus.

#202. I don't have time to sift through hundreds of resumes. How can I find a few good employee candidates to interview?

One often-overlooked source of information is the Internet. Instead of performing elaborate background checks, look to see if your applicant is registered on the social networking sites—LinkedIn, Facebook, and Twitter—and do a quick Google search as well. This free, preliminary glimpse at applicants will help you narrow the field as you get a sense of the person's personality and contacts. If they post racist or off-color jokes, for instance, you might want to think twice about allowing that person to represent your company.

#203. Beyond their basic qualifications, what should I look for when I interview job applicants?

You always want to surround yourself with positive individuals who can support you and your business. Try to get an idea of how they spend their time, and with whom. A record of volunteering, for instance, can indicate that they are people of character who care about the less fortunate.

Also, listen for clues regarding their attitude toward life. It sounds corny, but you don't want to hire people who seem depressed or angry. Your business needs, and deserves, the good energy of people who live in a world of possibilities, not a world of doom.

#204.   **Which questions should I ask (and avoid asking) in a job interview?**

The general rule for staying out of trouble when interviewing prospective employees is, don't ask personal questions. You may not ask about the candidate's religion, political affiliations, or marital or parenting status. Your aim is to learn whether the person is the best candidate for the job.

Do ask for professional references, and ask the person why those particular references were chosen. Check with at least one reference to verify employment dates, job duties, whether the person was reliable, and special skills. Also, ask if they would hire the person again.

#205.   **I've never had employees before. What are some management styles that work well for small businesses?**

These three management styles are considered effective and are easily applicable to small businesses:

1. **Participatory style.** For this style to work, all staff must see their roles as essential and equally important elements of the team. They should feel free to give their input and should be encouraged to "own" their part of the project. When they do a job well, or even show enthusiasm for the work, you should thank them and encourage them further.
2. **Directing style.** This top-down approach gives you authority over all players, work distribution, decisions, and ultimately, responsibility for success or failure of a project. You set the standards and clear goals, and you direct and orchestrate the work along the way.
3. **Teamwork style.** This style is participatory, but differs from the first style in that staff pool their knowledge, rather than be

mini-managers over their work. It is a give-and-take process that clarifies all expectations and logistics.

#206. How can I assess management styles and develop the best one for my office?

If you're managing a staff for the first time, don't overthink this question and research a dozen management styles. Confine your thoughts to the three outlined here, and ask yourself the following questions:

- Do you want to share the company's news and progress with your employees, or would you rather keep those details to yourself?
- Are you open to suggestions about how the company is run?
- Do you want to be friends with your staff, sharing information about your private lives?
- Do you enjoy boosting other peoples' self-confidence?
- Are you the type of person who needs to take all the credit for a shared effort you directed, as well as all the blame?
- Are you inclined to pay your staff more as the business becomes more profitable?
- Do you need to closely supervise people, or are you happy to trust that they will do their jobs?

#207. What are the traits and best practices of a good boss?

The good boss concentrates on being effective, and on upgrading his employees' skills so that they will be as effective as possible, too. He leaves his staff alone to do their job, is willing to both teach and learn from his staff, thanks and praises them appropriately, and neither spies on his workers nor throws them under the bus.

More than anything, he is honest. He shares business strategies with the staff, sees them as colleagues, and lets them know when something isn't working—and why. He's a good listener, communicator, and mentor.

#208.   How can I build morale among my staff?

One approach some entrepreneurs have taken is open-book accounting, a highly inclusive situation where staff are informed about all company records and decisions. It can be a highly successful managerial tool, but if you don't want to confide in your staff to that extent, a gesture such as a monthly "mental health day-off incentive" can show that you care about them as people. Think about their individual interests; you might reward a tennis buff with two tickets to an important tournament, or a Kindle owner with an Amazon gift card for new books. Even thanking them often, and telling them you appreciate their efforts can go a long way toward building morale.

#209.   I can't afford to give my staff raises this year. How can I reward them without spending much money?

Extra time off works. You also can provide gifts that are substantial but would cost less than a raise, such as gym memberships, paid parking, or even a paid vacation, such as a four-day cruise.

#210.   What is your best idea for a low-cost employee incentives?

One of the most meaningful incentives is a professional development opportunity, to show the staffer that he is so valuable to the business, you're willing to invest in his future in order to keep his skills sharp. Consider sending your best employees to occasional conferences where they will learn more about the latest technologies and trends in your field, and where they can practice networking with other professionals in similar businesses.

#211. I only have four employees. Do I need an employee manual?

While an employee manual or handbook isn't a legal requirement, it's good place to set down clearly defined employment policies. The expectations of employers and employees are too complex to recite, and standards for workplace behavior should be described as explicitly as possible. As a practical matter, manuals also help prevent employee lawsuits.

#212. What are the most important points that I should include in an employee manual?

Your manual should be comprehensive, covering as many aspects of being employed by you as possible. As a self-employed person, you may be tempted to operate a more relaxed office and deal with situations as they arise, rather than setting down policies in a manual. That approach, however, isn't very businesslike; should something unpleasant develop with an employee, it's much better to point to a policy and hold the other person accountable.

Basic elements of an employee manual include:

- Policies regarding absenteeism, tardiness, working hours, breaks, vacation days, holidays, and other benefits.
- Policies regarding appearance, grooming, attitude, and confidentiality.
- Rules about food, drink, cigarette smoking, alcohol usage, and substance abuse in the office (or outside the office, if

you choose), as well as personal telephone usage, and other at-work behaviors.

- Policies regarding sexual harassment.
- Expense reimbursement policies.
- General statements defining staff positions and their duties.
- List of funds usually withheld from paychecks, such as payroll taxes and insurance.

#213. How do I determine pay and benefits for my employees?

Learn what the market is paying. You should pay a competitive salary in order to attract and keep good staff, and your trade association should have information from recent salary surveys to guide you.

Another useful resource is Salary.com *(www.salary.com)*. Among this website's offerings is a "Salary Wizard;" simply enter a job title and zip code and you can view pay ranges, benefits packages and other particulars for similar positions in your town.

Job responsibilities and wages will vary across the country and between companies, but those sources will give you an idea.

#214. Any ideas for fine-tuning the question of how much to pay?

Look to the person's potential value to you. How does that job compare to others in the company? Examine benefits as well—would the candidate be willing to accept more vacation time in lieu of higher pay? And do you really need this work done by a full-time employee? Using the services of an independent contractor—a self-employed person such as yourself—or a part-time employee could save you money.

#215. **What is the official difference between an independent contractor and an employee?**

A contractor is someone who provides goods or services under terms that are specified in a contract. A contractor doesn't work "regularly" for a company, except when such regular work is expressed or implied in the written agreement.

Trying to pass off an employee as a contractor, just to save yourself the expense of a higher salary and benefits, is illegal and will cause you big problems with the IRS. If you have any doubts as to whether someone working for you should be classified as a contractor or an employee, call the IRS and ask them.

#216. **When is it better to hire a contractor, instead of an employee?**

If the core competency required by this position is necessary to your business, try to hire an employee. If the skills are expendable, or aren't needed every day for optimal operations, then try using a contractor.

#217. **How much should I pay an independent contractor?**

With few exceptions, independent contractors are paid either by the job (a flat fee), or by the hour. Talk to your colleagues in your trade association and Monday breakfast group and get an idea of what contractors for particular jobs are paid in your area.

You can also find some info online for paying contractors. Your best bet is to go to a search engine such as *www.google.com* and type a phrase such as, "fees, freelance writer" (6 million results) or "fees, self-employed piano teacher" (110,000 results) in the search box.

#218. I work from home, and have two part-time assistants who also work from their homes. What's a practical way to update them on trends and get their ideas?

Once every month or two, hold a half- or full-day "retreat." You can rent an office space and have breakfast or lunch catered or just meet at your home office if the area is suitable. Prepare a specific agenda, including your thoughts on how well your current arrangements are working and how your processes might be streamlined. Think of your agenda as an inverted pyramid—start with "big" issues and ideas relating to your entire industry, and schedule those issues pertaining to just the three of you at the end of the list. Keep it upbeat; focus on improvements for the future rather than complaints about how things were done before. Leave plenty of time for questions and ideas from your assistants.

#219. Are there specific techniques for firing an employee?

Firing someone is always tough, but if you must do it, be precise in communicating the reasons. Enumerate them clearly. Don't give the employee an opportunity to dispute the reasons or to beg for another chance for personal reasons. Assuming you followed your own policies and exhausted all other disciplinary options, calling someone into your office to be fired should be an irrevocable, non-negotiable decision. Apologize once but state that this is a necessary move and that you wish the person well in their future endeavors. If the employee becomes emotional, don't stay and engage or even express further sympathy; simply state that you'll give the person a little privacy and leave the room.

　　You can ease up on the stern demeanor for a layoff, but do make it a serious meeting—no joking or laughing. And don't insult the employee by saying how difficult this is for you; you're not the one getting the boot. If the worker asks why he or she is being laid off, answer truthfully. For both firings and layoffs, come to the meeting prepared; anticipate the worker's questions and objections and, especially in a firing, bring any supporting documents you might need, such as the employee's absentee records.

#220. Is outsourcing a good move for small businesses? What are the pros and cons?

Outsourcing can be a great problem solver for self-employed people with too much on their plates. Not only do you buy a freelancer's time, you also buy her talents and expertise. As long as you make sure she continually updates her tech skills, she could become one of your most relied-on consultants.

Outsourcing gives you a way to control costs because you're not hiring the person full-time with benefits, and a good outsourcing company can begin work on your project right away. Working with such independents frees you to focus on your business—and, incidentally, chances are you'll be giving work to another self-employed person!

There are disadvantages too, however. You might not want to hand over part of your operations to someone who works elsewhere, and you need to be sure you can trust the outsourcer with company information. (Many businesses require outside workers to sign a nondisclosure agreement that carries legal penalties for divulging company information.) If you're working with a large outsourcing firm, find out about language barriers. Many such firms hire workers in faraway lands who can be difficult to understand on the phone.

#221. What kinds of jobs work well when outsourced?

The easiest jobs to outsource are those that

- Require no special equipment, such as editorial services or picture framing

- Require no supervision
- Can be paid for by the hour, such as customer service, or by the product or volume, such as boxes assembled

Think of outsourcing as hiring freelancers or "remote workers" who may be sole proprietors such as yourself. Jobs often outsourced include graphic or website design, marketing and public relations, translating, transcribing services, an answering service, report writing, performing background or reference checks, market research, tax consulting, bookkeeping, collections, and various editorial services—which, increasingly, includes blogging for companies.

#222. How do I obtain genuine feedback from customers, or otherwise learn how unsupervised employees are doing?

There are six main avenues for getting reliable customer feedback:

1. Ask customers if they're satisfied with the product and service, either by directly asking when you see them, or by customer-opinion postcards or table tents.
2. Be a customer yourself, or recruit a friend or relative to be a "mystery shopper."
3. Assemble a focus group, up to ten individuals (preferably not your friends or relatives) who will give honest answers to questions about their experience with your business. You can find an easy-to-understand article on conducting a focus group at *www.managementhelp.org*.
4. Conduct a brief survey. The most economical survey venue is online.
5. Keep reliable statistics about your company, and how and when customers use it.
6. Talk to your front-line staff about customer and client reactions. Staff often don't want to convey negative information to

their boss, so they'll need to understand that this is an important part of your job.

#223.   I'm ready to take my business to the next level, but I can't decide whether to buy or start a second business, or to build on my current success by expanding. How do I decide?

When you aren't sure what the "next level" would be, it might make more sense to expand or diversify, rather than open a new business. After all, could you replicate the experience of the first business when you aren't even sure where it should take you next?

These basic thoughts should clarify some of your doubts:

1. First, identify what you're sure you don't want to do, such as expand to other cities.
2. Do you want to stay in one location, no matter what? If the answer is "yes," then your next question will be, "Okay, then what?"
3. Consider that what you're craving might simply be a more satisfying work environment, or a more profitable enterprise. In that case, you have many options; you could even diversify into seven businesses in one location.
4. List the businesses you could possibly spin off from your current businesses, if you had more space under one roof. For example, if you currently own a coffee shop, you could branch into catering, a gourmet bakery, a coffee roasting business, and a deli—all the while keeping your same brand and ownership. All of the businesses would support the others. Keep the list going until you run out of ideas. Play with it over the next few weeks and decide what touches you, which new skills you could (or would) learn, and how much you can afford.

#224.   As a self-employed person, is it ever okay to turn down work?

There's an acronym among self-employed people about unpleasant clients: PITA, or Pain In The A##. Not only is it acceptable to walk away from their work, it's a waste of time to stay with them. Time spent trying to please PITA clients is time you could invest in looking for better clients, or working for current ones who enhance your work life. Do yourself a favor and end overly stressful client relationships.

#225.   I own an online shop, and I've had a few PITA customers—are they always right?

One advantage of doing business online is that you really don't have to face customers. That gives you an edge when both of you are angry, because you can keep your scowl hidden from the public view.

When you read an e-mail from an angry customer, it's only natural to feel defensive and angry in return—but don't respond right away. Instead, leave your office for ten minutes. Take a brief walk outside or watch a talk show while you take deep breaths and force yourself to smile.

When you feel calm again, go back to your computer and read the angry e-mail. You will see that the message wasn't personal; the customer was complaining about one of your products or services. Offer a resolution to the problem and, if you're not sure whether you were able to keep your anger out of the message, ask an assistant or friend for their opinion before you send your response.

#226.   What is "passive income," and how can I earn some?

Passive income refers to money you can earn without actually performing a service for a client, or selling a product. In the answer to the next question, I've included some websites that might help you earn passive income. Possibilities include:

- **Affiliate links:** Many website owners insert links to other sites; when one of your readers clicks on a link to another site, you've just made a referral—and if your referral buys something at that other website, you earn a small percentage.
- **Website ads:** You allow an ad to appear on your blog or website. Like affiliate links, when one of your readers clicks on the ad and buys something at that site, you earn a few cents.
- **Sell products with your logo:** If you think people would buy a coffee mug, tote bag, or t-shirt showing off your design or company logo, you can upload your designs to any number of ad-product sites that produce and sell such items. When people buy "your" products, you get a check.
- **Sell stock photos:** You only need take the photo once and place it with a stock photo site. You lose control over who publishes your photos, but you receive royalties on them into the future.
- **Sell reprints of your published writing:** Once you've had a story or article published, you can sell reprints (if you retained rights to the piece) to any additional magazines or newspapers you wish. Reprint sales pay only a fraction of the original sale price, and sending your articles around to multiple outlets is a lot of work, but for many writers it pays off.

#227. **What are some of the websites and other outlets where I can earn passive income?**

For affiliate links, register as an affiliate at *www.amazon.com* and *www.barnesandnoble.com*. You can recommend books or other products on your site, and sales of it at Amazon or B&N—made by your readers after clicking on your links—will be credited to you.

For passive ad income, the most popular is AdSense, a Google ad program for people who want to place ads on their blogs and websites. At times your site can become a bit cluttered with ads, but that's the trade-off.

And if you think clients (or at least your mom) will buy items with your designs or logo, a good site for selling them is *www .cafepress.com*. You decide which products will carry your design and you can sell up to 80 items. CafePress automatically pays you when someone makes a purchase.

For stock photos, check out *www.alamy.com*; this website is used by many professional photographers.

#228.   What is the "Lean" concept of management?

Lean is a management practice that was popularized by Toyota. The basic concept is that expending any resources—time, dollars, energy, human effort, and movement—to create anything except the end value for customers is wasteful. It has since been applied to every field from insurance firms to municipal court systems.

#229.   How can I apply the Lean principles to my home-based business?

The best way to apply the Lean system is to look at your office or business through the "Seven Wastes" on which Lean is based;

1. **Rework**. Customers cannot accept a defective product, so the effort to create the initial product was wasted.
2. **Overproduction**. Each time you produce more than customers need or will buy, effort and materials were wasted.
3. **Transportation**. Moving a product risks damaging it, losing it, or delaying its delivery, in addition to transportation costs that really add no value to the product.

4. **Waiting.** When workers wait for resources to arrive, resources are wasted all along the production and delivery chain.
5. **Inventory.** Whether it refers to raw materials or finished products, inventory produces no value for customers. If it's not being actively processed, it is waste.
6. **Motion.** When a worker or equipment takes unnecessary steps, time and money are wasted.
7. **Overprocessing.** When you use a resource that is more expensive or valuable than necessary for the value of the product, money is wasted.

#230. **I've heard of people working in a "paperless office." How could I achieve that?**

It's not likely that you can, though I do know self-employed people who maintain all-paperless transactions. In the book, *The Myth of the Paperless Office*, authors Abigail J. Sellen and Richard H. R. Harper recommend finding a way to optimize our use of both paper and electronic communications. By cutting back on paper—by photocopying less, using only recycled paper, copying on both sides of paper, and reading newspapers and magazines online (free of charge, in most cases)—we can green our offices and help save the planet.

#231. **How important is it to thank outsiders who do positive things for my business, and what are some affordable ways to do that?**

It's extremely important to thank people who help you, whether it's with their advice, wisdom, talents, or something more tangible.

For small favors, an e-mail or thank-you card will suffice. Flowers, food gifts, or tickets to a sporting event are all generic gifts that will impress the recipient. For a special touch, give something that coincides with the person's individual interests, such as a one-day cooking class or a donation in their name to their favorite charity.

#232.   **I'm a person who tries to anticipate difficulties of all kinds. How do I know if hard times are ahead for my business?**

It's always good to be prepared for possible difficulties down the road. A slump in business is impossible to predict, but you can be alert for a few clues: Are your clients cutting back in purchasing your products or services? Are your vendors or suppliers having problems?

If you sense a slowdown in the future, here are a few suggestions:

- Talk with experienced, successful entrepreneurs in your trade association, and to friends who are self-employed.
- Don't be complacent. Have alternative providers in mind, in case yours are unable to fulfill your needs for any reason, and always be proactive in searching for new clients. It takes time to build relationships.
- The experts say, be strategic now, not reactionary later. You can't make good financial decisions during a crisis.

#233.   **What are Small Business Development Centers, and how can they help a struggling small business?**

The Office of Small Business Development Centers, an arm of the SBA offers management assistance to anyone who owns a small business or is interested in starting one. What each center offers is tailored to its community, and area businesspeople and educators donate their time and expertise. Services include financial counseling, marketing assistance, organization, engineering, technical services, procurement assistance, and training in various areas of small business management, from research reports on various industries to personal guidance.

More than 1,000 branches of the Small Business Development Centers program are located across the country, many on college campuses. To find one near you, go to *www.sba.gov /aboutsba/sbaprograms/sbdc*.

#234. **Are there ways to protect my business in hard times?**

Realize that when the economy is slow, people shift from making big purchases to buying smaller treats. Offer more of those; if your business is a hair salon, offer deals on haircuts or manicures because people will be cutting back on the $150 hair coloring jobs.

#235. **Is it a bad idea to launch new products and services in tough economic times?**

When the economy slows down, retailers carry fewer products and manage their inventory more closely, so think twice about launching new products or increasing production, even if your sales are good. It's not such a major issue when you consider offering a new service, but in producing and selling new products, you want to be cautious about exposing your business to major risks.

#236. **If I do go ahead and launch a new product, how can I maximize its chances for success?**

Put an effort into creating a buzz about your new product. Announce it one to two months before it will be unveiled at major trade shows; that way prospective clients will be expecting the product and will look for it. And be ready to let the product go if the timing of your launch is off.

#237. **Are there other ways to distinguish my business in hard times, so cash-strapped customers won't forget about me?**

Focus on a new service, and try to forget short-term profits for a while. If your business is home repairs, toss in an hour of free house-related consulting with every repair job for a month. During the holiday season, almost any business—including home-based consultants and other freelancers—can offer gift certificates; send an e-mail "blast" to clients to announce the certificates.

#238. **How can I be sure my business will still be here after a crisis?**

You can't be sure, but you can maximize your chances by remembering that cash is king, and saving all you can now, before a crisis happens.

Why is cash king? In an economic slump, cash is more difficult to get. Banks stop making loans and credit rates soar. Individuals and businesses stop using credit because it's too expensive; they can't keep up with their payments.

So, building and maintaining a healthy cash reserve will put you in a stronger position than your competitors who have no cash. You will be able to purchase your office supplies, including those obscenely expensive printer ink cartridges, and keep your business going. If your computer or other equipment breaks down, you'll have the resources to repair it. You might even take a few risks—but only a few—with slow-paying clients who will show their loyalty when the economy is strong again.

In other words, with cash in hand, you will be able to manage cash flow. You should conserve your cash, then and now, but don't hoard it.

Never be complacent, particularly about marketing. Be the one to create the "new fresh thing," instead of sitting back and watching your customer base diminish. And get your customers to pay you sooner with incentives, such as a 5 percent discount if they pay in full up front.

#239. **I work long hours; how can I keep up with new technologies that could change the way I work?**

This can be an excellent opportunity to get involved with your trade association. On a local or national level, most associations offer seminars and "boot camps" to help members keep up with the latest technology in your field. Take advantage of these offerings when you can; they're also a great time for networking.

#240. **Can my home-based business be successful if I only work at it part-time?**

That depends on what you mean by "successful" and "part-time." If you aren't looking for a full-time income from your business, yes, it can be a success if you only work at it part-time.

#241. **Can I expect to make more money as a sole proprietor than I earned in my past life as an employee? How often does that happen?**

Sole proprietors who charge competitive rates and keep costs down can earn a very comfortable living, depending on their location, career, expenses, and the current state of the economy. But it's not always possible, especially during your first few years of self-employment, to earn that much. Keep in mind the new expenses that didn't exist when you were an employee, such as office supplies and equipment, association fees, admission to networking events, and everyone's favorite—individual health insurance.

Still, it's important not to put up obstacles in your path. When I first started writing as a sole proprietor, I was amazed to learn that it was possible to earn a six-figure income doing this. I even met a few self-employed writers who had passed the quarter-million-dollar mark. They weren't famous novelists; in fact, some of them were ghostwriters whose names never appeared in print. They were just individuals who knew how to work efficiently and go after high-paying clients. Needless to say, I spent as much time with them as I could, listening and learning.

#242. **Is it possible to promote my new business too much?**

Probably not—but it *is* possible to be unprepared for a super-successful promotion campaign. I remember a restaurant review that I wrote about ten years ago, raving about the tasty food and hearty portions in a new, "calorie-conscious" restaurant in Cleveland, OH. Unfortunately, the day after my review was published, about 150 hungry customers showed up for lunch at the small diner, and nearly 100 of them had to be turned away.

Try to envision a marketing surge that's *too* successful. If you run out of whatever you're selling—whether it's consulting time, a service, or a product—how will you handle those customers who were shut out? An IOU can be a positive solution, if you can fulfill it within a reasonable time.

#243. **What are some more cost-cutting tips for the self-employed person?**

You can save dollars by encouraging your staff to work from home, thereby cutting your utility costs. Get into low-cost marketing techniques using the Internet, such as blogs, webcasts, and podcasts.

Another new trend is the sharing of staff between two businesses. You might be able to share secretarial services, your bookkeeper, or other employees with another small business.

#244. **What else could I share with other small businesses to cut costs?**

Try collaborating with them on office or commercial space. A dress shop and stationery store could be compatible in the same space. Or, you could free up some cash by buying supplies together and getting a bigger discount. But both parties need to make their expectations clear before you begin; the first time one party is late with their payment, the relationship could be tainted.

#245. **What is succession planning, and when should I start thinking about it?**

Succession planning is the process that will determine successors for various positions in the business, including your own. It involves recruitment and training, and you should begin thinking about it now, especially if yours is a family business. It can be a complex and emotional process; if your trade association doesn't currently offer seminars in succession planning, suggest that they add this topic to their offerings.

#246. **How can I drive in more business during slow periods?**

Offer package deals, possibly two-for-one purchases, or discounts for repeat buys. If your return policy is restrictive, soften it and issue a press release announcing the new policy. And invest a little more time in building relationships with clients, so they will refer you more often.

#247. How can my small business compete against large firms and chains?

Offer them something they won't find at the "big box" outlets— better deals, tastier coffee, free delivery even if they're just buying a single item, and personalized service. And remember their names.

Think of a way to solve a problem for your customers. With free delivery, for instance, you're saving them some time. Sending coffee shop gift cards to valued clients on their birthdays adds a bit of convenience to their lives, and they're guaranteed to smile when they open the envelope—and they'll think of your business when they use the gift card.

#248. Is it appropriate to ask for an advance at the beginning of a big project?

Absolutely. Either one-third or one-half of the total price is the standard, with the remaining money due on acceptance of the final product. Talk with your colleagues to see which option is usually used in your profession.

#249. How should I respond when a prospective client wants free work before hiring me?

Offer to provide samples of past projects, along with a list of current and former clients. Everyone has to crank out proposals that may or may not bring in a client, but working on spec isn't acceptable once you're a professional.

#250. **I need a "signature" for my services—
some small touch that will make clients remember
me and, perhaps, mention me to their friends.
Any suggestions?**

Flowers are the best way to energize a room and make someone
smile, and they're affordable at supermarkets. Give yours a special touch by attaching a card printed with your business's mission
statement. If you need help writing the perfect mission statement,
go to *www.missionstatement.com* for advice and examples.

Afterword

For self-employed people, "cocktail conversation" inevitably means answering the question, "How do you work for yourself? I wouldn't have the nerve to quit my job."

But self-employment has to work for me because I no longer have the nerve to scrape the ice off my windshield, drive through nasty weather and face a boss every morning before the sun comes up. Financial uncertainty no longer scares me, but the notion of giving up control over my work life—no longer choosing my clients, setting my own fees, making my own schedule, or lingering over breakfast—makes me shudder.

If you picked up this book, you're already on that path. You've at least begun to visualize your life as a business owner—the biggest hurdle! Everything else can be learned and practiced. If I did my job well, then this book has taught you that the missing pieces in your background are at your fingertips. They're not that difficult to master, and you will find plenty of agencies, associations, and individuals waiting to help you succeed.

One of my favorite authors, Brenda Ueland, wrote, "We are always afraid to start something that we want to make very good, true, and serious." Ms. Ueland knew, and you will discover, that you can do this. Self-employment stopped being a wispy fantasy long ago; it is a straightforward but deeply rewarding journey toward your highest career goals.

I wish you wild success in self-employment! Be brave, be calm, and believe in yourself. And let's follow each other on Twitter: I'm @marymihaly.

SAMPLE CONTRACT

This is a simple agreement letter that I've used many times with clients. It's the sort of agreement I ask clients to sign when they hire me to perform editorial services, but the various points are applicable to a wide variety of services.

I've adjusted it over the years to try to anticipate surprises. You can find many more samples of contracts on the web.

Agreement to Write Material for Happy Company Website

Mary Mihaly, Writer/Editor, and Sally Happy, Principal of Happy Company, agree to the following:

1. Mary Mihaly will write three (3) short articles, not to exceed 200 words each, on "Healthy Cookies" topics, using material provided by Sally Happy and according to Happy's specifications.
2. Mary Mihaly will copyedit three (3) short articles, not to exceed 300 words each, provided by Sally Happy, on Healthy Cookies and the Happy Company.
3. Mary Mihaly will edit ten (10) feature-length health-related articles provided by Sally Happy and according to Happy's specifications.
4. Mary Mihaly will complete the above-specified writing and editing by the end of business hours on Friday, May 15, 2009,

or approximately two weeks from the date on this document. If for any reason Mihaly cannot make that deadline, she agrees to notify Sally Happy immediately.

5. In addition to the above-specified writing and editing, Mary Mihaly agrees to one complete revision of the copy produced under this agreement, if necessary.

6. Sally Happy agrees to pay Mary Mihaly an advance payment of Two Thousand Dollars ($2,000.00) immediately on signing this agreement.

7. Sally Happy agrees to pay Mary Mihaly an additional Three Thousand Dollars ($3,000.00) within 15 days of acceptance and approval of the copy produced under this agreement. If the copy produced by Mary Mihaly is deemed not acceptable after one revision, Sally Happy is under no obligation to make the final $3,000.00 payment to Mary Mihaly.

8. By signing this agreement, Mary Mihaly forfeits all rights to copy produced under this agreement and accepted and approved by Sally Happy. All rights to copy produced under this agreement that is accepted and approved by Sally Happy, belong to Happy Company. If the copy produced under this agreement are not accepted and approved by Sally Happy, then rights to the copy remain with Mary Mihaly.

9. If copy produced under this agreement is accepted and approved by Sally Happy, then Happy agrees to present the next Happy Company writing and/or editing opportunity to Mary Mihaly, who will have first right of refusal.

_____

(Signature, Mary Mihaly, date)

_____

(Signature, Sally Happy, date)

THE 250 QUESTIONS

Part 1: The Decision and Getting Started

1: Which personal qualities do I need to be successfully self-employed?

2: How do I know if I'm self-motivated enough to be a business owner?

3: Which job benefits will I lose when I become self-employed?

4: What are some financial pluses of being self-employed?

5: What are some other advantages of self-employment—especially if I'm working from a home office?

6: I want to work from home. How do I decide what kind of business to start?

7: What are the most popular home-based businesses?

8: How will I know when to quit my day job and start my new business?

9:   Is starting a business in a tough economy a bad decision?

10:   Why do so many people want to run their own businesses?

11:   I haven't told my spouse that I want to start my own business and work from home. What issues should I bring up in that conversation?

12:   What is the survival rate for a new small business?

13:   What are the top reasons home-based businesses fail?

14:   What kind of small business will be successful?

15:   What is the biggest challenge facing small businesses?

16:   What type of business can I start with little or no capital?

17:   I keep hearing about the "informal economy," or "hidden economy." What is that and is it a good way for me to start my self-employment?

18:   How much money will I need to start my business?

19:   Where do self-employed people find the money to start their businesses?

20:   What is the SBA's (Small Business Administration's) start-up loan program, and what can the SBA do for me?

21:   Do I need a mentor, and where would I find one?

22:   Do I need an accountant to start or buy my own business?

23: Do I need an attorney in order to start or buy my own business?

24: When and how should I set up bookkeeping for my new business?

25: What is a business plan, and what should mine include?

26: What should I know if I'm opening a store online?

27: What are the major pros and cons of buying an existing business?

28: I'd like to buy an existing business. Where do I search for a good one?

29: How do I research a company that interests me?

30: Can I approach business owners directly, to ask if they are interested in selling?

31: Is there a formula to help determine a fair price for a business?

32: What are some advantages and disadvantages of buying a franchise?

33: What is a master franchise? A franchise fee? A franchise royalty?

34: How can I know if my business would make a successful franchise?

35: Do you have any tips to help my franchise succeed?

Part 2: The Office

36:   Do I need major office equipment—printer, copier, fax, postage meter—for my home office?

37:   I'm not a techie. How do I choose a computer for my new small business?

38:   What are the pros and cons of purchasing reconditioned computers and other office equipment?

39:   What are the pros and cons of leasing, rather than purchasing, office equipment?

40:   What is the most efficient way to arrange my office?

41:   My office is being overrun with documents. How do I avoid the inevitable reams of records?

42:   I've set up my home office, but frankly, it's a depressing space. Any tips for transforming it into a place I'll enjoy and can be productive every day?

43:   I want to "go green" with my business. How can my office reflect my concern for the environment?

44:   Where can I find decent office furniture without spending too much money?

45:   How do I find discounts on office supplies?

46:   What are some easy techniques for organizing files and paperwork?

47:   I keep a lot of newsletters and magazines for reference. How can I cut down on that clutter?

48: What is the ideal space for a home-based office?

49: I don't have an actual spare room for my new home-based business. How can I create a dedicated workplace in another room?

50: Clients will be visiting my office. How can I give it a professional appearance?

51: I manage with my office in the dining room, but I need to meet with clients from time to time. Any ideas?

52: I've heard of home offices being shut down for zoning violations. How do I avoid such a catastrophe?

53: I'll have a part-time assistant for my home-based business. How can I find a space for her in my very small office?

54: Could I find a VA to do more technical work?

55: Is taking a home-office deduction on my income taxes a "red flag" to Internal Revenue Service auditors?

Part 3: Financial and Legal Aspects

56: What does my personal credit score have to do with being self-employed?

57: How do I learn my credit score and credit history?

58: What is the best way to establish credit for my new business?

59: Should I have separate bank accounts and credit cards for my business?

60: Where can I get a grant to start my business?

61: Do I need to draw up contracts for the services I provide to my clients?

62: Should I use bookkeeping software? How do I choose the right one?

63: Is there a formula for estimating my projected business expenses?

64: What kind of insurance coverage do I need for a home-based business?

65: Does my homeowner's insurance cover my home-based business?

66: What's my personal liability as a sole proprietor, and what protection do I need?

67: What insurance do I need for a small business not based at home—say, an auto repair shop or coffee shop?

68: Where can I find affordable health insurance as a self-employed person?

69: What is a Health Savings Account (HSA)?

70: What's the difference between tangible, intangible, and intellectual property?

71: How can I protect my intellectual property?

72: Define a "sole proprietorship." How do I know that's the best business structure for me?

73: I'm a sole proprietor—when should I consider incorporating?

74: What does it take to incorporate?

75: What is an S corporation? What are the advantages of becoming one?

76: What's the difference between a limited partnership and a general partnership?

77: Are a limited partnership and a limited liability company (LLC) the same thing?

78: What if I start a partnership and later decide I can't work with my partners?

79: What are business incubators?

80: Do I need an operating license for my home-based business?

81: Will I need a vendor's license for my new business?

82: How do I register (or otherwise protect) the name of my new business?

83: How should I handle billing my clients?

84: What steps should I take if payment is overdue?

85: Should I sue a nonpaying client in Small Claims Court?

86: What do "business cash flow" and "net after-tax income" mean?

87: What are gross profit and net profit?

88: I don't know anything about accounting, but I don't want that to stop me from launching my business. Where can I find a simple tutorial?

89: I'm a sole proprietor. Should I use a Federal ID number or Individual Taxpayer Identification Number (ITIN) in the business, instead of my Social Security number?

90: What does it mean to "certify" my business, and what are the advantages?

91: When does the IRS consider me self-employed?

92: What is self-employment tax?

93: Who must pay self-employment tax?

94: Do self-employed people have to pay federal income tax, Medicare tax, and/or unemployment tax?

95: What is a W-2 form and do sole proprietors need one?

96: What is a 1099 form and would a self-employed person need one?

97: What are asset depreciation and amortization?

98: What are some typical home-office deductions?

99: How does an independent contractor claim business deductions?

100:   As a self-employed person, can I form a 401(k) retirement plan?

101:   What's the difference between a Roth, Traditional, and SEP Independent Retirement Account (IRA)?

102:   What are the advantages and disadvantages to opening a Roth IRA?

103:   What are the advantages and disadvantages to opening a Traditional IRA?

104:   What are the advantages and disadvantages to opening a SEP IRA?

105:   When and how will I start drawing from the IRAs I've opened?

106:   What other options for retirement savings do self-employed people have?

107:   I keep hearing the phrase, "pay yourself first." What does that mean?

108:   Where should a self-employed person invest her retirement funds—in real estate, mutual funds, CDs, or elsewhere?

109:   What retirement options should a small business offer its employees?

110:   This retirement business is confusing. Where can a small business owner find (cheap, free) help with financial planning for herself and her business?

111: How much Social Security income will be available to me by the time I retire?

Part 4: Marketing and Selling Your Products and Services

112: What's the difference between advertising, marketing, and public relations?

113: What is a marketing plan, and why does a self-employed person need one?

114: What are the elements of an effective marketing plan?

115: How do I write a press release, and where do I send it?

116: Do I need a website for my business? Why?

117: What is a domain name, and where do I get one? Can I use it for e-mail, too?

118: What is the best marketing tool for a home-based business?

119: How do I build an affordable website? What will it cost me?

120: Are e-newsletters good marketing tools? What are the benefits?

121: How do I set up my e-newsletter?

122: What would I write in an e-newsletter?

123: How do I build a mailing list for my e-newsletter and other online promotions?

124: Are blogs valuable for a business?

125: What's the difference between an e-newsletter and a blog?

126: How can I use e-mail to market myself?

127: I don't want to send spam—are there guidelines for sending bulk e-mail, such as newsletters?

128: How can I be sure my e-mails won't be deleted before someone reads them?

129: When is it appropriate to use abbreviations in business-related e-mail?

130: What should I know about protocol and professionalism in business-related e-mail?

131: What are the legal ramifications of what I write in an e-mail?

132: What is networking, and why is it important to someone working alone in a home office?

133: How can I tweak my website to make it a great place where people return, again and again?

134: How do I get people to visit my website in the first place?

135: How else can I use the Internet to promote my new business?

136: What is LinkedIn, and how do I join?

137: What is Facebook, and how do I join?

138: What is Twitter, and how do I join?

139: I'm a shy person. What are some easy, in-person ways to network?

140: I'm not a "joiner." Why do I need to join trade associations?

141: I'd like to talk to those with self-employed success stories in my field. Any tips for gaining access to them?

142: How should I view my competitors? I'm not an aggressive person, but I don't want to feel intimidated by the competition, either.

143: How do I distinguish my business from others that provide essentially the same products or services?

144: As a self-employed person, do I need a logo for my business?

145: How do I design or choose a memorable business card?

146: When are other kinds of promotional items—bookmarks, scratch pads, pens—useful?

147: Are there any unusual ways of networking or marketing myself that my competitors don't know about?

148: What is "viral marketing"? It sounds contagious.

149: How will I know the ROI (return on investment) for my networking efforts?

150:    How can I improve the outcomes of my networking?

151:    How often should I update my contact lists and mailing lists? Are there easy ways to do that job?

152:    How do I set fees for my services?

153:    What does "branding" mean? Why is it important?

154:    How can I get my clients to refer me to other prospective clients?

155:    Do you have a networking tip that will increase my business?

156:    When are thank-you gifts for clients appropriate?

157:    How can I get publicity for my new business?

158:    What is strategic networking?

159:    How do I engage prospective clients?

160:    If a prospective client's needs seem urgent or troublesome, how can I secure them as a client without waiting for months?

161:    I've never advertised before—are there basic advertising guidelines for promoting my product or services?

162:    How do I hire salespeople when I don't have a background in sales?

163:    How and where can I learn some sales basics?

164: How do I become more visible in my community? Will that help my business?

165: How do I find clubs and other organizations that would invite me to speak at their meetings and events?

166: How do I approach clubs and other organizations to offer my services as a speaker?

167: Are there other ways to give to the community that might also be good for business?

168: Why should I get on the board of trustees of a nonprofit organization?

169: How do I become a board member?

170: What's the best way to handle customer complaints?

171: I spend way too much time in servicing small customers. How can I learn about more efficient customer service?

Part 5: Time, Energy, and Personal Considerations

172: I'm a sole proprietor, working out of my home—where can I find others to share ideas with?

173: I just set up my home office. How can I keep my family from coming in here and disturbing me all the time?

174: How can I tactfully handle friends and family who think that because I'm self-employed, I'm always available?

175: How can I handle friends and family who expect free or discounted services just because I'm self-employed?

176: As a sole proprietor, I feel as if I'm working all the time, and I feel guilty if I take time off. How can I balance my personal and business lives?

177: How can I stay focused and enthusiastic about my new business?

178: I need to exercise, but can't leave my home office for two hours to go to the gym. How can I exercise at home, and incorporate it into my work day?

179: Working from my home office, I don't eat right anymore and often feel sluggish. How can I keep my energy high?

180: I'm easily distracted, and I know the TV in the next room will be a constant temptation. How do I discipline myself to work all day?

181: Now that I'm working at home, how can I minimize the feeling of isolation that sometimes creeps in?

182: How can I motivate myself to network when I don't feel like it?

183: I have two employees—how do I motivate them to network? Are there motivational tools I can offer them?

184: How can I get better at remembering people's names?

185: Where can I learn to be a good negotiator?

186: I want to get out there and promote my business. How do I get over my fear of public speaking?

187: How can I learn to be a better public speaker?

188: I run a family business. How do I keep family relations separate from business issues?

189: Should I start a business with my spouse? What are the pitfalls of a husband/wife business?

190: Is it a good idea to hire other family members, such as adult children?

191: What are some tips, day by day, that will help me prevent burnout and keep me feeling balanced?

192: How can I keep my clients in an economic downturn? I can't afford to charge them less.

193: I find I can't run my home-based business alone. Can a college intern help me?

194: What kind of work could an intern do for me?

195: I want to start a catering business in my home. Where can I learn about health ordinances, inspections, and other regulations that would affect me?

196: Should I set regular business hours for my new company?

197: I'm a single parent with a child at home. Can I realistically start a home-based business now, or should I wait until my kid is in school?

Part 6: Managing Ongoing Success

198: Aside from watching my checking account grow, how should I evaluate the success of my business?

199: How can I self-evaluate my performance as the owner and leader of my business?

200: How do I know if self-employment is still the best choice for my life?

201: When should I hire employees for my home-based business?

202: I don't have time to sift through hundreds of resumes. How can I find a few good employee candidates to interview?

203: Beyond their basic qualifications, what should I look for when I interview job applicants?

204: Which questions should I ask (and avoid asking) in a job interview?

205: I've never had employees before. What are some management styles that work well for small businesses?

206: How can I assess management styles and develop the best one for my office?

207: What are the traits and best practices of a good boss?

208: How can I build morale among my staff?

209: I can't afford to give my staff raises this year. How can I reward them without spending much money?

210:   What is your best idea for low-cost employee incentives?

211:   I only have four employees. Do I need an employee manual?

212:   What are the most important points that I should include in an employee manual?

213:   How do I determine pay and benefits for my employees?

214:   Any ideas for fine-tuning the question of how much to pay?

215:   What is the official difference between an independent contractor and an employee?

216:   When is it better to hire a contractor, instead of an employee?

217:   How much should I pay an independent contractor?

218:   I work from home, and have two part-time assistants who also work from their homes. What's a practical way to update them on trends and get their ideas?

219:   Are there specific techniques for firing an employee?

220:   Is outsourcing a good move for small businesses? What are the pros and cons?

221:   What kinds of jobs work well when outsourced?

222:   How do I obtain genuine feedback from customers, or otherwise learn how unsupervised employees are doing?

223: I'm ready to take my business to the next level, but I can't decide whether to buy or start a second business, or to build on my current success by expanding. How do I decide?

224: As a self-employed person, is it ever okay to turn down work?

225: I own an online shop, and I've had a few PITA customers—are they always right?

226: What is "passive income," and how can I earn some?

227: What are some of the websites and other outlets where I can earn passive income?

228: What is the "Lean" concept of management?

229: How can I apply the Lean principles to my home-based business?

230: I've heard of people working in a "paperless office." How could I achieve that?

231: How important is it to thank outsiders who do positive things for my business, and what are some affordable ways to do that?

232: I'm a person who tries to anticipate difficulties of all kinds. How do I know if hard times are ahead for my business?

233: What are Small Business Development Centers, and how can they help a struggling small business?

234: Are there ways to protect my business in hard times?

235: Is it a bad idea to launch new products and services in tough economic times?

236: If I do go ahead and launch a new product, how can I maximize its chances for success?

237: Are there other ways to distinguish my business in hard times, so cash-strapped customers won't forget about me?

238: How can I be sure my business will still be here after a crisis?

239: I work long hours; how can I keep up with new technologies that could change the way I work?

240: Can my home-based business be successful if I only work at it part-time?

241: Can I expect to make more money as a sole proprietor than I earned in my past life as an employee? How often does that happen?

242: Is it possible to promote my new business too much?

243: What are some more cost-cutting tips for the self-employed person?

244: What else could I share with other small businesses to cut costs?

245: What is succession planning, and when should I start thinking about it?

246: How can I drive in more business during slow periods?

247: How can my small business compete against large firms
      and chains?

248: Is it appropriate to ask for an advance at the beginning of
      a big project?

249: How should I respond when a prospective client wants
      free work before hiring me?

250: I need a "signature" for my services—some small touch
      that will make clients remember me and, perhaps,
      mention me to their friends. Any suggestions?

INDEX

Accountants, 17–18
Accounting tutorials, 59–60
AdSense, 136
Advances, 144
Advertising, 73, 98
Amortization, 63
Asset depreciation, 63
Attorneys, 18

Bank accounts, 47
Ben & Jerry's, 72
Billing, 58
Blogs, 79–80, 84
Board membership, 100–101
Bookkeeping, 19
Bookkeeping software, 48
Boss, 125–26
Branding, 94
Breakfast, 109

Burnout, 115
Business. *See also* Home-based businesses;
    Small businesses
    buying an existing, 8, 21–24
    distinguishing your, 89–90
    establishing credit for, 46
    expansion, 133
    managing successful, 120–45
    reasons to start, 9
    start-ups, and economic downturns, 8
Business cards, 90–91
Business cash flow, 59
Business deductions, 63
Business expenses, estimating, 48–49
Business hours, 117
Business incubators, 56
Business licenses, 56–57

Business name, 57
Business plan, 19–20
Business structures, 53–56

CafePress, 136
Capital, 13–17
Cash flow, 59
Cash reserves, 7
Catering businesses, 117
Certified businesses, 60
Certified public accountants (CPAs), 18
Challenges, 12–13
Chamber of commerce, 88
Charitable giving, 100
Clients
    billing, 58
    difficult, 134
    meeting with, 39–40
    prospective, 97
    thank-you gifts for, 95–96
    turning down work from, 134
Clubs, 99–100
Clutter, 37
Colleagues, 105, 108, 110
Collections, 58–59
Community involvement, 99, 100
Competitors, 89, 144
Computers, 31–32
Consulting services, 7, 13
Contact lists, 93
Contracts, 48
Copiers, 31
Copyright, 52–53
Corporate culture, 6
Corporations, 53–55
Cost-cutting tips, 142–43
Credit cards, 47

Credit score, 45–46
Customer complaints, 101–02
Customer feedback, 132–33
Customer service, 13, 102

Dell, Michael, 72
Difficulties, preparing for future, 138
Discounts, 107, 116, 143
Distractions, 109
Documents, 33–34, 37
Domain names, 76
Dress code, 5

Earnings, 141–42
E-commerce, 20–21
Economic downturns, 8, 116, 139, 140–41
E-mail, 80–83
Employee manuals, 127–28
Employees
    building morale in, 126
    family members as, 114–15
    firing, 130–31
    hiring, 122–24
    incentives for, 126–27
    vs. independent contractors, 129
    managing, 124–26
    meetings with, 130
    motivating, 111
    pay and benefits for, 128
Energy level, 109
E-newsletters, 77–80
Evans, Bob, 72
Exercise, 108
Existing business, buying an, 8, 21–24
Expansion, 133

Facebook, 85, 86
Failure, reasons for, 10–12
Family
    affect of business on, 9–10
    as employees, 114–15
    limit setting with, 105–07
Family businesses, 113–14
Federal ID number, 60
Fee setting, 93–94, 116
Fictitious name, 57
Files, organizing, 37
Financial benefits, 5
Financial issues, 12–13, 44
Financial security, 10

Fire insurance, 51
Firings, 130–31
Flexibility, 5
Flowers, 145
401(k) retirement plans, 64
Franchise fee, 26
Franchises
    advantages and disadvantages of, 24–25
    master, 25–26
    successful, 26–27
    tips for, 27
Friends, limit setting with, 106–07
Funds
    lack of, 11
    start-up, 14–17

General liability insurance, 51
General partnerships, 55–56
Grants, 47
Green offices, 35
Gross profit, 59

Health insurance, 4, 49, 51–52
Health ordinances, 117
Health Savings Accounts (HSA), 52
Hidden economy, 14
Home-based businesses
    choosing type of, 6
    reasons for failure of, 10–12
    types of, 7, 13
Home office
    advantages of, 5–6
    clients visiting, 39
    green, 35
    location for, 34, 38–39
    setup, 30, 33–34
    zoning laws and, 40
Home-office deduction, 41, 47, 63
Homeowner's insurance, 49–50
Hypercommuting, 91

IKEA, 36
Impatience, 11
Income expectations, 141–42
Income taxes, 61–62
Income tax returns, 34
Incorporation, 53–54
Independent contractors, 129
Individual Retirement Accounts (IRAs),
    64–66

Individual Taxpayer Identification Number (ITIN), 60
Informal economy, 14
Insurance, 49–52
Intangible property, 52
Intellectual property, 52–53
Internal Revenue Service (IRS), 60–61
Interns, 116–17
Investors, 16
Isolation, 110

Job applicants, 123–24
Job benefits, 4

Late payments, 58–59
Lean management, 136–37
Leasing equipment, 32
Legal issues, 44
Liability, 50
Licenses, 14, 56–57
Life insurance, 49
Limited liability companies (LLCs), 56
Limited partnerships, 55–56
Limit setting, 105–07
LinkedIn, 85
Loans, 16–17
Local organizations, 99–100
Logos, 90

Magazines, 37
Mailing lists, 78–79, 93
Management styles, 124–25
Marketing, 11, 72–77, 80, 91–92, 142
Marketing plans, 73–74
Master franchise, 25–26
Medicare tax, 61–62
Meeting spaces, 39–40
Mentors, 17
Micro loans, 16
Money, start-up, 14–17
Morale building, 126
Motivation, 3–4, 104, 108, 110–11

Names, remembering, 111–12
Negotiation skills, 112
Net after-tax income, 59
Net profit, 59
Networking, 83, 87–88, 91–97, 110–11
New products, 139
Newsletters, 37

Niche business, 89–90
Nonprofit organizations, 100–101
Nutrition, 109

Office. *See also* Home office
  clients visiting, 39
  paperless, 137
Office assistants, 41–42
Office equipment, 31–32
Office furniture, 36
Office setup, 30, 33–34
Office space, rented, 38–39
Office supplies, 36–37
Online stores, 20–21, 134
Operating licenses, 56–57
Organization, 37
Outsourcing, 131–32

Paperless offices, 137
Paperwork, organizing, 37
Partnerships, 55–56
Part-time work, 141
Passive income, 134–36
Peer-to-peer loans, 16
Permits, 57
Persistence, 3–4
Personal liability, 50
Personal qualities, 3
Planning, 11
Press releases, 74–75
Printers, 31
Privacy, 38
Promotional items, 91
Property insurance, 49
Prospective clients, 97
Publicity, 96
Public relations (PR), 73
Public speaking, 99–100, 112–13

Reconditioned equipment, 32
Record keeping, 19, 33–34, 37
Referrals, 95
Retirement plans, 64–69
Roth IRAs, 64–65

Salaries, 128
Sales, 99
Salespeople, 98
Scanners, 33
Schedule, flexible, 5

Schedule SE, 61
S corporations, 55
Search engine optimization (SEO), 84
Self-discipline, 11–12
Self-employed persons, qualities of, 3
Self-employment
    advantages of, 5–6
    appeal of, 9
    assessing choice of, 122
    financial benefits of, 5
    IRS and, 60–61
Self-employment tax, 61
Self-evaluation, 121–22
Self-motivation, 3–4, 104
SEP IRAs, 64, 65–66
Service Corps of Retired Executives
    (SCORE), 17
Shyness, 87
Signature service, 144–45
Single parents, 117–18
Slowdowns, 138–41, 143
Small Business Administration (SBA),
    16–17
Small Business Development Centers,
    138–39
Small businesses
    challenges facing, 12–13
    reasons for failure of, 10–12
    successful, 12
    survival rate for new, 10
    types of, 13
Small claims court, 58–59
Social entrepreneurs, 90
Socializing, 105
Social networking, 85–86
Social Security, 68, 69
Social Security number, 60
Sole proprietorships, 53–54
Spam, 81
Spec work, 144
Spouse, 9–10, 114
Startup money, 14–17
Stewart, Martha, 72
Storage, 33
Strategic networking, 96–97
Succession planning, 143
Surveys, 92

Tangible property, 52
Tax audits, 41

Tax deductions, 41, 47, 63
Taxes, 34, 61–62
Technology, 141
1099 forms, 62
Thank yous, 95–96, 137
Time management, 107
Trade associations, 88, 105, 141
Twitter, 85, 86

Unemployment tax, 62

Vendor's license, 57
Viral marketing, 92
Virtual assistants (VAs), 41–42
Volunteering, 99

W-2 forms, 62
Websites, 75–77, 83–85
Worker's compensation insurance, 51
Work hours, 10, 109
Work-life balance, 107

Zoning laws, 7, 40

ABOUT THE AUTHOR

Mary Mihaly has been a self-employed full-time freelancer since 1993. She has written six books and more than 600 articles for national publications such as *Reader's Digest*, *Playboy*, *Yoga Journal*, *Continental*, *House Beautiful*, *Industry Week*, *Wall Street Journal*, *USAToday*, and many more.